M000086534

# TABLE OF CONTENTS

# Top 20 Test Taking Tips

1. Carefully follow all the test registration procedures
2. Know the test directions, duration, topics, question types, how many questions
3. Setup a flexible study schedule at least 3-4 weeks before test day
4. Study during the time of day you are most alert, relaxed, and stress free
5. Maximize your learning style; visual learner use visual study aids, auditory learner use auditory study aids
6. Focus on your weakest knowledge base
7. Find a study partner to review with and help clarify questions
8. Practice, practice, practice
9. Get a good night's sleep; don't try to cram the night before the test
10. Eat a well balanced meal
11. Know the exact physical location of the testing site; drive the route to the site prior to test day
12. Bring a set of ear plugs; the testing center could be noisy
13. Wear comfortable, loose fitting, layered clothing to the testing center; prepare for it to be either cold or hot during the test
14. Bring at least 2 current forms of ID to the testing center
15. Arrive to the test early; be prepared to wait and be patient
16. Eliminate the obviously wrong answer choices, then guess the first remaining choice
17. Pace yourself; don't rush, but keep working and move on if you get stuck
18. Maintain a positive attitude even if the test is going poorly
19. Keep your first answer unless you are positive it is wrong
20. Check your work, don't make a careless mistake

# Quantitative

## Number Sense

### Numbers and their Classifications

There are several different kinds of numbers. When you learn to count as a child, you start with *Natural Numbers*. You may know them as counting numbers. These numbers begin with 1, 2, 3, and so on. *Whole Numbers* are all natural numbers and zero. *Integers* are all whole numbers and their related negative values (...-2, -1, 0, 1, 2...).

Aside from the number 1, all natural numbers are known as prime or composite. *Prime Numbers* are natural numbers that are greater than 1 and have factors that are 1 and itself (e.g., 3). On the other hand, *Composite Numbers* are natural numbers that are greater than 1 and are not prime numbers. The number 1 is a special case because it is not a prime number or composite number. *Rational numbers* include all integers, decimals, and fractions. Any terminating or repeating decimal number is a rational number.

Numbers are the basic building blocks of mathematics. These terms show some elements of numbers:

Integers – The set of positive and negative numbers. This set includes zero. Integers do not include fractions $\left(\frac{1}{3}\right)$, decimals (0.56), or mixed numbers $\left(7\frac{3}{4}\right)$.

Even number – Any integer that can be divided by 2 and does not leave a remainder. Example: 2, 4, 6, 8, etc.

Odd number – Any integer that cannot be divided evenly by 2. For example: 3, 5, 7, 9, and so on.

Decimal number – a number that uses a decimal point to show the part of the number that is less than one. Example: 1.234.

Decimal point – a symbol used to separate the ones place from the tenths place in decimals. This symbol is used to separate dollars from cents in currency.

Decimal place – the position of a number to the right of the decimal point. In the decimal 0.123, the 1 is in the first place to the right of the decimal point. This is the place for tenths. The 2 is in the second place. This is the place for hundredths. The 3 is in the third place. This is the place for thousandths.

The decimal, or base 10, system is a number system that uses ten different digits (0, 1, 2, 3, 4, 5, 6, 7, 8, 9). Another system is the binary, or base 2, number system. This system is used by computers and uses the numbers 0 and 1. Some think that the base 10 system started because people had only their 10 fingers for counting.

**Place Value**

*Write the place value of each digit in the following number: 14,059.826*

> 1: ten thousands
> 4: thousands
> 0: hundreds
> 5: tens
> 9: ones
> 8: tenths
> 2: hundredths
> 6: thousandths

**Writing Numbers in Word Form**

<u>Example 1</u>
*Write each number in words.*

29: twenty-nine
478: four hundred seventy-eight
9,435: nine thousand four hundred thirty-five
98,542: ninety-eight thousand five hundred forty-two
302, 876: three hundred two thousand eight hundred seventy-six

<u>Example 2</u>
*Write each decimal in words.*

0.06: six hundredths
0.6: six tenths
6.0: six

0.009: nine thousandths;
0.113: one hundred thirteen thousandths;
0.901: nine hundred and one thousandths

**The Number Line**

A number line is a graph to see the distance between numbers. Basically, this graph shows the relationship between numbers. So, a number line may have a point for zero and may show negative numbers on the left side of the line. Also, any positive numbers are placed on the right side of the line. Before you work with negative numbers, you need to understand absolute values. Basically, a number's *Absolute Value* is the distance away from zero that a number is on the number line. The absolute value of a number is always positive and is written as $|x|$. If a number like -4 is added with a +2, then the sum is -2. So, the absolute value of $|-2|$ is +2.

*Example 1*
Name each point on the number line below:

Use the dashed lines on the number line to identify each point. Each dashed line between two whole numbers is $\frac{1}{4}$. The line halfway between two numbers is $\frac{1}{2}$.

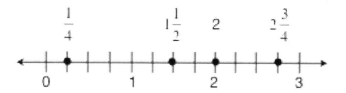

➢ **Review Video: <u>Numbers and Their Classification</u>**
*Visit **mometrix.com/academy** and enter **Code: 461071***

## Listing Numbers: Least to Greatest

<u>Example 1</u>
*4,002; 280; 108,511; 9*
Answer: 9; 280; 4,002; 108,511

<u>Example 2</u>
*5,075,000,600; 190,800,330; 7,000,300,001*
Answer: 190,800,330; 5,075,000,600; 7,000,300,001

## Rounding

Rounding is lowering the digits in a number and keeping the value similar. The result will be less accurate. However, this will be in a simpler form and will be easier to use. Whole numbers can be rounded to the nearest ten, hundred or thousand. Also, fractions and decimals can be rounded to the nearest whole number.

<u>Example 1</u>
Round each number to the nearest ten: 11 | 47 | 118

When rounding to the nearest ten, anything ending in 5 or greater rounds up.
So, 11 rounds to 10 | 47 rounds to 50 | 118 rounds to 120.

<u>Example 2</u>
Round each number to the nearest hundred: 78 | 980 | 248

When rounding to the nearest hundred, anything ending in 50 or greater rounds up.
So, 78 rounds to 100 | 980 rounds to 1000 | 248 rounds down to 200.

Example 3
Round each number to the nearest thousand: 302 | 1274 | 3756

When rounding to the nearest thousand, anything ending in 500 or greater rounds up.
So, 302 rounds to 0 | 1274 rounds to 1000 | 3756 rounds to 4000.

Example 4
Round each number to the nearest whole number: $\frac{5}{8}$ | 2.12 | $\frac{14}{3}$

When rounding fractions and decimals, anything half or higher rounds up.
So, $\frac{5}{8}$ rounds to 1 | 2.12 rounds to 2 | $\frac{14}{3}$ rounds to 5.

# Decimals, Fractions, and Percents

## Decimals

Decimal Illustration
Use a model to represent the decimal: 0.24. Write 0.24 as a fraction.

The decimal 0.24 is twenty four hundredths. One possible model to represent this fraction is
to draw 100 pennies, since each penny is worth 1 one hundredth of a dollar. Draw one
hundred circles to represent one hundred pennies. Shade 24 of the pennies to represent the
decimal twenty four hundredths.

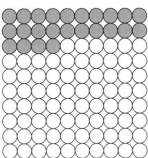

To write the decimal as a fraction, write a fraction: $\frac{\#\ shaded\ spaces}{\#\ total\ spaces}$. The number of shaded

spaces is 24, and the total number of spaces is 100, so as a fraction 0.24 equals $\frac{24}{100}$. $\frac{24}{100}$ can

then be reduced to $\frac{6}{25}$.

Adding and Subtracting Decimals
When adding and subtracting decimals, the decimal points must always be aligned. Adding
decimals is just like adding regular whole numbers.
Example: 4.5 + 2 = 6.5.

If the problem-solver does not properly align the decimal points, an incorrect answer of 4.7
may result. An easy way to add decimals is to align all of the decimal points in a vertical

column visually. This will allow one to see exactly where the decimal should be placed in the final answer. Begin adding from right to left. Add each column in turn, making sure to carry the number to the left if a column adds up to more than 9. The same rules apply to the subtraction of decimals.

> **Review Video: <u>Adding and Subtracting Decimals</u>**
> *Visit **mometrix.com/academy** and enter **Code: 381101***

<u>Multiplying Decimals</u>
A simple multiplication problem has two components: a multiplicand and a multiplier. When multiplying decimals, work as though the numbers were whole rather than decimals. Once the final product is calculated, count the number of places to the right of the decimal in both the multiplicand and the multiplier. Then, count that number of places from the right of the product and place the decimal in that position. For example, 12.3 x 2.56 has three places to the right of the respective decimals. Multiply 123 x 256 to get 31488. Now, beginning on the right, count three places to the left and insert the decimal. The final product will be 31.488.

> **Review Video: <u>Multiplying Decimals</u>**
> *Visit **mometrix.com/academy** and enter **Code: 731574***

<u>Dividing Decimals</u>
Every division problem has a divisor and a dividend. The dividend is the number that is being divided. In the problem 14 ÷ 7, 14 is the dividend and 7 is the divisor. In a division problem with decimals, the divisor must be converted into a whole number. Begin by moving the decimal in the divisor to the right until a whole number is created. Next, move the decimal in the dividend the same number of spaces to the right. For example, 4.9 into 24.5 would become 49 into 245. The decimal was moved one space to the right to create a whole number in the divisor, and then the same was done for the dividend. Once the whole numbers are created, the problem is carried out normally: 245 ÷ 49 = 5.

> **Review Video: <u>Dividing Decimals</u>**
> *Visit **mometrix.com/academy** and enter **Code: 560690***

**Fractions**

A fraction has one integer that is written above another integer with a dividing line between them $(\frac{x}{y})$. It represents the quotient of the two numbers "$x$ divided by $y$." Also, this can be thought of as $x$ out of $y$ equal parts. The x and y in this fraction are known as variables. When the value for a symbol can change, a variable is given to that value. So, a number like 3 is a constant. A value that does not change is a constant.

The top number of a fraction is called the numerator. This number stands for the number of parts. The 1 in $\frac{1}{4}$ means that this is one part out of the whole. The bottom number of a fraction is called the denominator. This stands for the total number of equal parts. The 4 in $\frac{1}{4}$ means that the whole has four equal parts. A fraction cannot have a denominator of zero. This fraction is known as "undefined." The reverse of a fraction is known as the reciprocal. For example, the reciprocal of 1/2 is 2, and the reciprocal of 3 is 1/3.

Fractions can be changed by multiplying or dividing the numerator and denominator by the same number. This will not change the value of the fraction. You cannot do this with addition or subtraction. If you divide both numbers by a common factor, you will reduce or simplify the fraction. Two fractions that have the same value but are given in different ways are known as equivalent fractions. For example, $\frac{2}{10}, \frac{3}{15}, \frac{4}{20}$, and $\frac{5}{25}$ are equivalent fractions. Also, they can be reduced or simplified to $\frac{1}{5}$.

Two fractions can be changed to have the same denominator. This is known as finding a common denominator. The number for the common denominator should be the least common multiple of the original denominators. Example: $\frac{3}{4}$ and $\frac{5}{6}$; the least common multiple of 4 and 6 is 12. So, you can change these fractions to have a common denominator: $\frac{3}{4} = \frac{9}{12}$ and $\frac{5}{6} = \frac{10}{12}$.

If two fractions have a common denominator, you can add or subtract the fractions with the two numerators. Example: $\frac{1}{2} + \frac{1}{4} = \frac{2}{4} + \frac{1}{4} = \frac{3}{4}$. If the two fractions do not have the same denominator, one or both of them must be changed to have a common denominator. This needs to be done before they can be added or subtracted.

Two fractions can be multiplied. The two numerators need to be multiplied to find the new numerator. Also, the two denominators need to be multiplied to find the new denominator. Example: $\frac{1}{3} \times \frac{2}{3} = \frac{1 \times 2}{3 \times 3} = \frac{2}{9}$. Two fractions can be divided. First, flip the numerator and denominator of the second fraction. Then multiply the numerators and denominators. Example: $\frac{2}{3} \div \frac{3}{4}$ becomes $\frac{2}{3} \times \frac{4}{3}$. Now, $\frac{8}{9}$ is your answer.

A fraction with a denominator that is greater than the numerator is known as a proper fraction. A fraction with a numerator that is greater than the denominator is known as an improper fraction. Proper fractions have values less than one. Improper fractions have values greater than one.

A mixed number is a number that has an integer and a fraction. Any improper fraction can be rewritten as a mixed number. Example: $\frac{8}{3} = \frac{6}{3} + \frac{2}{3} = 2 + \frac{2}{3} = 2\frac{2}{3}$.
Also, any mixed number can be rewritten as an improper fraction. Example: $1\frac{3}{5} = 1 + \frac{3}{5} = \frac{5}{5} + \frac{3}{5} = \frac{8}{5}$.

A fraction that has a fraction in the numerator, denominator, or both is called a *Complex Fraction*. These can be solved in many ways. The easiest way to solve the equation is to use order of operations.

For example, $\dfrac{\left(\frac{4}{7}\right)}{\left(\frac{5}{8}\right)} = \dfrac{0.571}{0.625} = 0.914$. Another way to solve this problem is to

multiply the fraction in the numerator by the reciprocal of the fraction in the denominator.
For example, $\dfrac{\left(\frac{4}{7}\right)}{\left(\frac{5}{8}\right)} = \dfrac{4}{7} \times \dfrac{8}{5} = \dfrac{32}{35} = 0.914$.

> **Review Video: <u>Fractions</u>**
*Visit **mometrix.com/academy** and enter **Code: 262335***

## Percentages

You can think of percentages as fractions that are based on a whole of 100. In other words, one whole is equal to 100%. The word percent means "per hundred." Fractions can be given as percents by using equivalent fractions with an amount of 100. Example:
$\dfrac{7}{10} = \dfrac{70}{100} = 70\%$; Another example is $\dfrac{1}{4} = \dfrac{25}{100} = 25\%$. To give a percentage as a fraction, divide the percentage by 100. Then, reduce the fraction to its simplest possible terms.
Example: $60\% = \dfrac{60}{100} = \dfrac{3}{5}$; $96\% = \dfrac{96}{100} = \dfrac{24}{25}$.

Converting decimals to percentages and percentages to decimals is as simple as moving the decimal point. To convert from a decimal to a percent, move the decimal point two places to the right. To convert from a percent to a decimal, move the decimal two places to the left. Example: $0.23 = 23\%$; $5.34 = 534\%$; $0.007 = 0.7\%$; $700\% = 7.00$; $86\% = 0.86$; $0.15\% = 0.0015$.

A percentage problem can come in three main ways.
- Type 1: What percentage of 40 is 8?
- Type 2: What number is 20% of 40?
- Type 3: What number is 8 20% of?

The three parts in these examples are the same: a whole (W), a part (P), and a percentage (%).
To solve type (1), use the equation % = P/W.
To solve type (2), use the equation: P = W × %.
To solve type (3), use the equation W = P/%.

Percentage Problems
Percentage problems can be difficult because many are word problems. So, a main part of solving them is to know which quantities to use.

*Example 1*
In a school cafeteria, 7 students choose pizza, 9 choose hamburgers, and 4 choose tacos. Find the percentage that chose tacos. To find the whole, you must add all of the parts: 7 + 9 + 4 = 20. Then, the percentage can be found by dividing the part by the whole (% = P/W):
$\dfrac{4}{20} = \dfrac{20}{100} = 20\%$.

*Example 2*

At a hospital, 40% of the nurses work in labor and delivery. If 20 nurses work in labor and delivery, how many nurses work at the hospital?

To answer this problem, first think about the number of nurses that work at the hospital. Will it be more or less than the number of nurses who work in a specific department such as labor and delivery? More nurses work at the hospital, so the number you find to answer this question will be greater than 20.

40% of the nurses are labor and delivery nurses. "Of" indicates multiplication, and words like "is" and "are" indicate equivalence. Translating the problem into a mathematical sentence gives $40\% \cdot n = 20$, where $n$ represents the total number of nurses. Solving for n gives $n = \frac{20}{40\%} = \frac{20}{0.40} = 50$.

Fifty nurses work at the hospital.

*Example 3*

A patient was given 40 mg of a certain medicine. Later, the patient's dosage was increased to 45 mg. What was the percent increase in his medication? To find the percent increase, first compare the original and increased amounts. The original amount was 40 mg, and the increased amount is 45 mg, so the dosage of medication was increased by 5 mg ($45 - 40 = 5$). Note, however, that the question asks not by how much the dosage increased but by what percentage it increased. Percent increase $= \frac{\text{new amount} - \text{original amount}}{\text{original amount}} \cdot 100\%$.

So, $\frac{45 \text{ mg} - 40 \text{ mg}}{40 \text{ mg}} \cdot 100\% = \frac{5}{40} \cdot 100\% = 0.125 \cdot 100\% \approx 12.5\%$

The percent increase is approximately 12.5%.

> ➤ **Review Video: Percentages**
> *Visit **mometrix.com/academy** and enter **Code: 141911**

**Converting Decimals to Fractions**

A fraction can be turned into a decimal and vice versa. In order to convert a fraction into a decimal, simply divide the numerator by the denominator. For example, the fraction $\frac{5}{4}$ becomes 1.25. This is done by dividing 5 by 4. The fraction $\frac{4}{8}$ becomes 0.5 when 4 is divided by 8. This remains true even if the fraction $\frac{4}{8}$ is first reduced to $\frac{1}{2}$. The decimal conversion will still be 0.5. In order to convert a decimal into a fraction, count the number of places to the right of the decimal. This will be the number of zeros in the denominator. The numbers to the right of the decimal will become the whole number in the numerator.

*Example 1:*

$0.45 = \frac{45}{100}$

$\frac{45}{100}$ reduces to $\frac{9}{20}$

*Example 2:*

$0.237 = \frac{237}{1000}$

*Example 3:*

$$0.2121 = \frac{2121}{10000}$$

> ➤ **Review Video: <u>Converting Decimals to Fractions and Percentages</u>**
> *Visit **mometrix.com/academy** and enter **Code: 986765***

# Operations

There are four basic operations in math: addition, subtraction, multiplication, and division.

Addition increases the value of one number by the value of another number. Example: 2 + 4 = 6; 8 + 9 = 17. The result is called the sum. With addition, the order does not matter. 4 + 2 or 2 + 4 equals 6. This is the commutative property for addition.

Subtraction decreases the value of one number by the value of another number. The result is called the difference. Example: 6 – 4 = 2 and 17 – 8 = 9. Note for subtraction that the order does matter. For example, 6 – 4 and 4 – 6 do not have the same difference.

Multiplication is like repeated addition. This operation tells how many times one number needs to be added to the other number. Example: 3 × 2 (three times two) = 2 + 2 + 2 = 6. With multiplication, the order does not matter. 2 × 3 (or 3 + 3) = 3 × 2 (or 2 + 2 + 2). This is the commutative property for multiplication.

Division is the opposite operation to multiplication. This operation shows how much of a number is in another number. The first number is known as the dividend. The second number is known as the divisor. The answer to the division problem is known as the quotient.
Example: 20 ÷ 4 = 5. If 20 is split into 4 equal parts, then each part is 5. With division, the order of the numbers does matter. 20 ÷ 4 and 4 ÷ 20 do not give the same result. Note that you cannot divide a number by zero. If you try to divide a number by zero, then the answer is known as undefined.

## Working with Positive & Negative Numbers

Addition: If the signs are the same, then add the absolute values of the addends and use the original sign with the sum. The addends are the numbers that will be added to have the sum. For example, $(+4) + (+8) = +12$ and $(-4) + (-8) = -12$. When the signs are different, take the absolute values of the addends and subtract the smaller value from the larger value. Then, put the original sign of the larger value on the difference. For example, $(+4) + (-8) = -4$ and $(-4) + (+8) = +4$.

Subtraction: For signed numbers, change the sign of the number after the minus symbol. Then, follow the same rules for addition. For example, $(+4)-(+8)$ becomes $(+4) + (-8) = -4$.

Multiplication: If the signs are the same, then the product is positive. For example, $(+4) \times (+8) = +32$ and $(-4) \times (-8) = +32$. If the signs are different, then the product is negative. For example, $(+4) \times (-8) = -32$ and $(-4) \times (+8) = -32$. When more than two factors are multiplied together, the sign of the product is decided by how many negative factors are in the equation. If there are an odd number of negative factors, then the product is negative. An even number of negative factors gives a positive product. For example, $(+4) \times (-8) \times (-2) = +64$ and $(-4) \times (-8) \times (-2) = -64$.

Division: The rules for dividing signed numbers are similar to multiplying signed numbers. If the dividend and divisor have the same sign, the quotient is positive. If the dividend and divisor have opposite signs, the quotient is negative. For example, $(-4) \div (+8) = -0.5$.

## Order of Operations

Order of Operations is a list of rules that gives the order of doing each operation in an expression. If you have an expression that with many different operations, Order of Operations tells you which operations to do first. An easy way to remember Order of Operations is PEMDAS.

This is written out as "Please Excuse My Dear Aunt Sally." PEMDAS stands for Parentheses, Exponents, Multiplication, Division, Addition, Subtraction. You need to understand that multiplication and division are equal as steps. Also, addition and subtraction are equal as steps. So, those pairs of operations are worked from left to right.

Example: Use order of operations for the expression $5 + 20 \div 4 \times (2 + 3)^2 - 6$.
**P**: Work on the operations inside the parentheses, $(2 + 3) = 5$.
**E**: Simplify the exponents, $(5)^2 = 25$.
The equation now looks like this: $5 + 20 \div 4 \times 25 - 6$.
**MD**: Work on multiplication and division from left to right, $20 \div 4 = 5$; then $5 \times 25 = 125$.
The equation now looks like this: $5 + 125 - 6$.
**AS**: Work on addition and subtraction from left to right, $5 + 125 = 130$; then $130 - 6 = 124$.

> ➤ **Review Video: Order of Operations**
> *Visit* ***mometrix.com/academy*** *and enter* ***Code: 259675***

## Estimation

Estimation is the process of finding an approximate answer to a problem. Estimation may involve rounding to the nearest whole number to make addition or subtraction easier.

*Example 1*
There are 24 people in an English class. Miss Foster decides to order three exam books for each student, plus 6 extras. She estimates that she should order 90 exam books. Identify if her solution is reasonable.

Write an expression to determine the total number of exam books to order. Since three books are ordered for each student, first multiply the number of books per student by the number of students: 3 books per student · 24 students = 72 books. Next, add the six extra exam books that Miss Foster would like to order. The total number of books to order is: 72 + 6 = 78 books. Her original estimate of 90 exam books is too large.

*Example 2*
The following food items are available in a school cafeteria for lunch:
Sandwich: $3.15; Soup: $1.84
Salad: $2.62; Pretzels: $0.95
Milk: $0.40

Daniel has $4.00 and wants to purchase a milk, sandwich, and soup. Emily has $4.00 and wants to purchase a salad, pretzels, and milk. Estimate the cost of each student's lunch and determine if they have enough money to purchase the food they would like for lunch.

Daniel wants to purchase a milk, sandwich, and soup. Rounded to the nearest fifty cents, the cost of his items is $0.50, $3.00, and $2.00. The total for his three items would be approximately:

$$0.50 + 3.00 + 2.00 = 5.50$$

It will cost Daniel approximately $5.50 for his lunch. He does not have enough money to purchase the items he has selected.

Emily wants to purchase a salad, pretzels, and milk. Rounded to the nearest fifty cents, the cost of her items is $2.50, $1.00, and $0.50. The total for her three items would be approximately:

$$2.50 + 1.00 + 0.50 = 4.00$$

It will cost Emily approximately $4.00 for her lunch. She has approximately enough money to purchase the items she has selected.

# Factors and Multiples

## Factors and Multiples

Factors are numbers that are multiplied for a product. An example is the equation $2 \times 3 = 6$. The numbers 2 and 3 are factors. A prime number has only two factors: 1 and itself. Other numbers can have many factors.

> ➤ **Review Video: Factors**
> *Visit **mometrix.com/academy** and enter **Code: 920086***

A common factor is a number that divides exactly into two or more numbers. For example, the factors of 12 are 1, 2, 3, 4, 6, and 12. The factors of 15 are 1, 3, 5, and 15. So, the common factors of 12 and 15 are 1 and 3. A prime factor is a factor that is a prime number. Thus, the prime factors of 12 are 2 and 3. For 15, the prime factors are 3 and 5.

The greatest common factor (GCF) is the largest number that is a factor of two or more numbers. For example, the factors of 15 are 1, 3, 5, and 15. The factors of 35 are 1, 5, 7, and 35. So, the greatest common factor of 15 and 35 is 5.

A multiple of a number is the product of the number and some other integer. Common multiples are multiples that are shared by two numbers. The least common multiple (LCM) is the smallest number that is a multiple of two or more numbers. For example, the multiples of 3 are 3, 6, 9, 12, 15, etc. The multiples of 5 are 5, 10, 15, 20, etc. Therefore, the least common multiple of 3 and 5 is 15.

> **Review Video: <u>Multiples</u>**
*Visit mometrix.com/academy and enter Code:* **626738**

## Ratios, Proportions, and Scale Drawings

<u>Ratios</u>
A ratio is a comparison of two numbers in a certain order. Example: There are 14 computers in a lab, and the class has 20 students. So, there is a student to computer ratio of 20 to 14. Normally, this is written as 20:14.

Ratios can be listed as *a to b*, *a:b*, or *a/b*. Examples of ratios are miles per hour (miles/hour), meters per second (meters/second), and miles per gallon (miles/gallon).

> **Review Video: <u>Ratios</u>**
*Visit mometrix.com/academy and enter Code:* **996914**

<u>Proportions and Cross Products</u>
A proportion is a relationship between two numbers. This relationship shows how one changes when the other changes. A direct proportion is a relationship where a number increases by a set amount with every increase in the other number.

Another way is for the number to decrease by that same amount for every decrease in the other quantity. Example: For every 1 sheet cake, 18 people can have cake. The number of sheet cakes and the number of people that can be served from them is a direct proportion.

Inverse proportion is a relationship where an increase in one number has a decrease in the other. This can work the other way where a decrease in a number has an increase in the other.
Example: The time needed for a car trip decreases as the speed increases. Also, the time for the trip increases as the speed decreases. So, the time needed for the trip is inversely proportional to the speed of the car.

Two equal ratios have cross products that are equal. This can be written as $\frac{m}{b} = \frac{w}{z}$. For example, Fred travels 2 miles in 1 hour, and Jane travels 4 miles in 2 hours. So, their speeds are proportional because $\frac{2}{1} = \frac{4}{2}$.

In a proportion, the product of the numerator of the first ratio and the denominator of the second ratio is equal to the product of the denominator of the first ratio and the numerator of the second ratio. In other words, you can see that $m \times z = b \times w$. So, $2 \times 2 = 1 \times 4$.

> ➤ **Review Video: <u>Proportions</u>**
> *Visit **mometrix.com/academy** and enter **Code: 505355***

<u>Actual Drawings and Scale Drawings</u>
A map has a key for measurements to compare real distances with a scale distance. Example: The key on one map says that 2 inches on the map is 12 real miles. Find the distance of a route that is 5 inches long on the map.

A proportion is needed to show the map measurements and real distances. First, write a ratio that has the information in the key. The map measurement can be in the numerator, and the real distance can be in the denominator.

$$\frac{2 \text{ inches}}{12 \text{ miles}}$$

Next, write a ratio with the known map distance and the unknown real distance. The unknown number for miles can be represented with the letter $m$.

$$\frac{5 \text{ inches}}{m \text{ miles}}$$

Then, write out the ratios in a proportion and solve it for $m$.

$$\frac{2 \text{ inches}}{12 \text{ miles}} = \frac{5 \text{ inches}}{m \text{ miles}}$$

Now, you have $2m = 60$. So, you are left with $m = 30$. Thus, the route is 30 miles long.

# Algebra, Functions, and Patterns

## Translating

Words to Mathematical Expression
Write "four less than twice $x$" as a mathematical expression.

Remember that an expression does not have an equals sign. "Less" indicates subtraction, and "twice" indicates multiplication by two. Four less than $2x$ is $2x - 4$. Notice how this is different than $4 - 2x$. You can plug in values for $x$ to see how these expressions would yield different values.

Words to Mathematical Equation
Translate "three hundred twenty-five increased by six times $3x$ equals three hundred forty-three" into a mathematical equation.

The key words and phrases are "increased by," "times," and "equals."
Three hundred twenty-five increased by six times $3x$ equals three hundred forty-three:
$325 + 6(3x) = 343$

The mathematical sentence is $325 + 6(3x) = 343$.

Mathematical Expression to a Phrase
Write a phrase which represents this mathematical expression: $75 - 3t + 14^2$.

Because there are many words which indicate various operations, there are several ways to write this expression, including "seventy-five minus three times $t$ plus fourteen squared."

## Roots and Square Roots

A root, or *Square Root*, is a number that when multiplied by itself gives a real number. For example, $\sqrt{4} = +2$ and $-2$ because $(-2) \times (-2) = 4$ and $(2) \times (2) = 4$. Now, $\sqrt{9} = +3$ and $-3$ because $(-3) \times (-3) = 9$ and $(3) \times (3) = 9$. So, +2 and -2 are square roots of 4. Also, +3 and -3 are square roots of 9.

Instead of using a superscript (e.g., $a^x$), roots use the radical symbol (e.g., $\sqrt{\phantom{x}}$) for the operation. A radical will have a number underneath the bar (i.e., radical symbol). Also, a number can be placed in the index. This is the upper left where $n$ is placed: $\sqrt[n]{a}$. So, this is read as *the $n^{th}$ root of a*. There are two special cases for the use of n. When n = 2, this is a square root. When n = 3, this is a cube root.

If there is no number to the upper left, it is understood to be a square root (n = 2). Almost all of the roots that you will face will be square roots. A square root is the same as a number raised to the $\frac{1}{2}$ power. When we say that a is the square root of b ($a = \sqrt{b}$), we mean that the variable multiplied by itself equals b: ($a \times a = b$).

A perfect square is a number that has an integer for its square root. There are 10 perfect squares from 1 to 100: 1, 4, 9, 16, 25, 36, 49, 64, 81, 100. These are the squares for integers: 1, 2, 3, 4, 5, 6, 7, 8, 9, and 10.

**Exponents and Parentheses**

A number like 7, 23, or 97 is a base number. A number that is connected to the base number like $7^3$, $23^4$, or $97^2$ is a superscript number. An exponent is a superscript number placed at the top right of a base number. Exponents are a short form of a longer math operation. This superscript number shows how many times the base number is to be multiplied by itself.

Example: $a^2 = a \times a$ or $2^4 = 2 \times 2 \times 2 \times 2$. A number with an exponent of 2 is said to be *squared*. A number with an exponent of 3 is said to be *cubed*. The value of a number raised to an exponent is called its power. So, $8^4$ is read as *8 to the 4th power* or *8 raised to the power of 4*. A negative exponent can be written as a fraction to have a positive exponent. Example: $a^{-2} = 1/a^2$.

<u>Laws of Exponents</u>
The laws of exponents are as follows:
1) Any number to the power of 1 is equal to itself: $a^1 = a$.
    - Examples: $2^1 = 2$ | $-3^1 = -3$
2) The number 1 raised to any power is equal to 1: $1^n = 1$.
    - Examples: $1^3 = 1$ | $1^{30} = 1$
3) Any number raised to the power of 0 is equal to 1: $a^0 = 1$.
    - Examples: $8^0 = 1$ | $(-10)^0 = 1$ | $(1/2)^0 = 1$
4) Add exponents to multiply powers of the same base number: $a^n \times a^m = a^{n+m}$.
    - Example: $2^3 \times 2^4 = 2^{3+4} = 2^7 = 128$
5) Subtract exponents to divide powers of the same base number: $a^n \div a^m = a^{n-m}$.
    - Example: $\frac{2^5}{2^3} = 2^{5-3} = 2^2 = 4$
6) When a power is raised to a power, the exponents are multiplied: $(a^n)^m = a^{n \times m}$.
    - Example: $(3^2)^3 = 3^2 \times 3^2 \times 3^2 = 3^6 = 729$
7) Multiplication and division operations that are inside parentheses can be raised to a power. This is the same as each term being raised to that power: $(a \times b)^n = a^n \times b^n; (a \div b)^n = a^n \div b^n$.
    - Multiplication: $(2 \times 3)^2 = 2^2 \times 3^2 = 4 \times 9 = 36$
    - Division: $(4 \div 3)^3 = 4^3 \div 3^3 = 64 \div 27 = 2.37$

Note: Exponents do not have to be integers. Fractional or decimal exponents follow all the rules above as well. Example: $5^{\frac{1}{4}} \times 5^{\frac{3}{4}} = 5^{\frac{1}{4}+\frac{3}{4}} = 5^1 = 5$.

> ➤ **Review Video: <u>Law of Exponents</u>**
> *Visit **mometrix.com/academy** and enter **Code: 532558***

Parentheses are used to show which operation should be done first when there is more than one operation. Example: $4 - (2 + 1) = 1$. So, the first step for this problem is to add 2 and 1. Then, subtract the sum from 4.

## Properties

The Commutative Property of Addition is shown here, which states that you can add terms in any order.
$$2x + y = y + 2x$$

The Distributive Property is shown here, which states that a number multiplied to an expression in parentheses must be multiplied to every term in the parentheses.
$$5 \times (x + 1) = (5 \times x) + (5 \times 1)$$

The Identity Property of Multiplication is shown here, which states that multiplying a number or term by 1 does not change its value.
$$3 \times 1 = 3$$

The Commutative Property of Multiplication is shown here, which states that you can multiply terms in any order.
$$6 \times m \times n = m \times n \times 6$$

The Associative Property of Multiplication is shown here, which states that any group of numbers and/or variables can be grouped together in parentheses to be multiplied first before multiplying by the remaining numbers and/or variables.
$$4 \times (5a) = (4a) \times 5$$

The Identity Property of Addition is shown here, which states that adding 0 to any number or term does not change the value of that number or term.
$$s + 0 = s$$

The Associative Property of Addition is shown here, which states that any group of numbers and/or variables can be grouped together in parentheses to be added first before adding the remaining numbers and/or variables.
$$10 + (6 + 1) = (10 + 6) + 1$$

### Coefficients and the Distributive Property

Coefficients
A coefficient is a number or symbol that is multiplied by a variable. For example, in the expression 2(ab), the number 2 is the coefficient of (ab). The expression can be written in other ways to have a different coefficient. For example, the expression can be 2a(b). This means that 2a is the coefficient of (b).

Distributive Property
The distributive property can be used to multiply each addend in parentheses. Then, the products are added to reach the result. The formula for the distributive property looks like this:
$$a(b + c) = ab + ac$$
Example: 6(2+4)
First, multiply 6 and 2. The answer is 12.
Then, multiply 6 and 4. The answer is 24.
Last, we add 12 and 24. So, the final answer is 36.

## Solving for a Variable

Similar to order of operation rules, algebraic rules must be obeyed to ensure a correct answer. Begin by locating all parentheses and brackets, and then solving the equations within them. Then, perform the operations necessary to remove all parentheses and brackets. Next, convert all fractions into whole numbers and combine common terms on each side of the equation.

Beginning on the left side of the expression, solve operations involving multiplication and division. Then, work left to right solving operations involving addition and subtraction. Finally, cross-multiply if necessary to reach the final solution.

*Example 1:*
$4a$-10=10

Constants are the numbers in equations that do not change. The variable in this equation is $a$. Variables are most commonly presented as either $x$ or $y$, but they can be any letter. Every variable is equal to a number; one must solve the equation to determine what that number is. In an algebraic expression, the answer will usually be the number represented by the variable. In order to solve this equation, keep in mind that what is done to one side must be done to the other side as well. The first step will be to remove 10 from the left side by adding 10 to both sides. This will be expressed as $4a$-10+10=10+10, which simplifies to $4a$=20. Next, remove the 4 by dividing both sides by 4. This step will be expressed as $4a \div 4 = 20 \div 4$. The expression now becomes $a$=5.

Since variables are the letters that represent an unknown number, you must solve for that unknown number in single variable problems. The main thing to remember is that you can do anything to one side of an equation as long as you do it to the other.

*Example 2:*
Solve for x in the equation 2x + 3 = 5.

Answer: First you want to get the "2x" isolated by itself on one side. To do that, first get rid of the 3. Subtract 3 from both sides of the equation 2x + 3 − 3 = 5 − 3 or 2x = 2. Now since the x is being multiplied by the 2 in "2x", you must divide by 2 to get rid of it. So, divide both sides by 2, which gives 2x / 2 = 2 / 2 or x = 1.

## Manipulating Equations

Sometimes you will have variables missing in equations. So, you need to find the missing variable. To do this, you need to remember one important thing: whatever you do to one side of an equation, you need to do to the other side. If you subtract 100 from one side of an equation, you need to subtract 100 from the other side of the equation. This will allow you to change the form of the equation to find missing values.

*Example*
Ray earns $10 an hour. This can be given with the expression $10x$, where $x$ is equal to the number of hours that Ray works. This is the independent variable. The independent variable is the amount that can change. The money that Ray earns is in $y$ hours. So, you would write the equation: $10x = y$. The variable $y$ is the dependent variable. This depends

on $x$ and cannot be changed. Now, let's say that Ray makes \$360. How many hours did he work to make \$360?

$$10x = 360$$

Now, you want to know how many hours that Ray worked. So, you want to get x by itself. To do that, you can divide both sides of the equation by 10.

$$\frac{10x}{10} = \frac{360}{10}$$

So, you have: $x = 36$. Now, you know that Ray worked 36 hours to make \$360.

**Functions**

*Example 1*
The table below is the value of each part of an ordered pair. An ordered pair is written as: (x, y)

| x | y |
|---|---|
| 2 | 6 |
| 4 | 12 |
| 6 | 18 |
| 8 | 24 |

You can find y if you know x. The number in the y column is three times the number in the x column. Multiply the x number by 3 to get the y number.

| x | y |
|---|---|
| 2 | 2 × 3 = 6 |
| 4 | 4 × 3 = 12 |
| 6 | 6 × 3 = 18 |
| 8 | 8 × 3 = 24 |

*Example 2*
The table shows some data points for a linear function. What is the missing value in the table?

| x | y |
|---|---|
| 0 | ? |
| 3 | 50 |
| 5 | 80 |

The data in the table represent a linear function. For a linear function, the rate of change is equal to the slope. To find the slope, calculate the change in $y$ divided by the change in $x$ for the two given points from the table: $m = \frac{80-50}{5-3} = \frac{30}{2} = 15$

The rate of change of the linear function is 15. This means for each increase of 1 in the value of $x$, the value of $y$ increases by 15. Similarly, each decrease of 1 in the value of $x$ decreases the value of $y$ by 15. The x-value 0 is 3 less than 3, so subtract $3 \cdot 15 = 45$ from 50 to get $y = 5$. This is the missing value in the table.

**Sequencing**

*Example 1*
Use the sequence to find each of the following.
6, 13, 20, 27, 34, 41, ...
a) Find the position of 34.
b) Find the value of the term in position 7.

a) The position of a term is its place in the sequence. The sequence begins with 6, in position 1, 13 is position 2, etc. The term 34 has a position of 5.

b) The terms in positions 1 through 6 are given. To find the term in position 7, identify the difference between each term.
13 – 6 = 7
20 – 13 = 7
27 – 20 = 7
34 – 27 = 7
41 – 34 = 7
The terms are increasing by 7. To find the 7th term, add 7 to the sixth term, 41:
41 + 7 = 48
The term in position 7 is 48.

*Example 2*
The $n$th term of a sequence is: $4n - 6$. Find the terms in position: 1, 4, and 10.

To find the terms in each given position, evaluate the expression for the $n$th term at the given position values.
1st term: $4(1) - 6 = 4 - 6 = -2$
4th term: $4(4) - 6 = 16 - 6 = 10$
10th term: $4(10) - 6 = 40 - 6 = 34$

*Example 3*
Write an algebraic expression to determine the $n$th term of the arithmetic sequence:
31, 25, 19, 13, ....

To find the $n$th term, find the common difference between each pair of given terms.
2nd term – 1st term: $25 - 31 = -6$
3rd term – 2nd term: $19 - 25 = -6$
4th term – 3rd term: $13 - 19 = -6$
The first term is 31, so when $n = 1$, the term is 31.
1st term: $31 + -6(n - 1)$

Simplify this expression and check it for terms 2, 3, and 4 by evaluating the expression at $n$ = 2, 3, and 4.
$31 + -6(n - 1) = 31 - 6n + 6 = -6n + 37$
2nd term: $-6(2) + 37 = -12 + 37 = 25$
3rd term: $-6(3) + 37 = -18 + 37 = 19$
4th term: $-6(4) + 37 = -24 + 37 = 13$
The $n$th term of the arithmetic sequence is $-6n + 37$.

# Geometry

## Lines and Planes

A point is a fixed location in space. This point has no size or dimensions. Commonly, this fixed location is a dot. A collinear point is a point which is on the line. A non-collinear point is a point that is not on a line.

A line is a set of points that go forever in two opposite directions. The line has length but no width or depth. A line can be named by any two points that are on the line. A line segment is a part of a line that has definite endpoints. A ray is a part of a line that goes from a single point and goes in one direction along the line. A ray has a definite beginning but no ending.

A plane is a two-dimensional flat surface that has three non-collinear points. A plane goes an unending distance in all directions in those two dimensions. This plane has an unending number of points, parallel lines and segments, intersecting lines and segments. Also, a plane can have an unending number of parallel or intersecting rays. A plane will never have a three-dimensional figure or skew lines. Two given planes will be parallel, or they will intersect to form a line. A plane may intersect a circular conic surface (e.g., a cone) to make conic sections (e.g., the parabola, hyperbola, circle, or ellipse).

Perpendicular lines are lines that intersect at right angles. The symbol $\perp$ stands for perpendicular lines. The shortest distance from a line to a point that is not on the line is a perpendicular segment from the point to the line.

Parallel lines are lines in the same plane that have no points in common and never meet. The lines can be in different planes, have no points in common, and never meet. However, the lines will not be parallel because they are in different planes.

A bisector is a line or line segment that divides another line segment into two equal lengths. A perpendicular bisector of a line segment has points that are equidistant (i.e., equal distances) from the endpoints of the segment.

Intersecting lines are lines that have exactly one point in common. Concurrent lines are several lines that intersect at a single point. A transversal is a line that intersects at least two other lines. The lines may or may not be parallel to one another. A transversal that intersects parallel lines is common in geometry.

## Coordinate Plane

Often, algebraic functions and equations are shown on a graph. This graph is known as the *Cartesian Coordinate Plane*. The Cartesian coordinate plane has two number lines that are perpendicular. These lines intersect at the zero point. This point is also known as the origin. The horizontal number line is known as the *x*-axis.

On the *x*-axis, there are positive values to the right of the origin and negative values to the left of the origin. The vertical number line is known as the *y*-axis. There are positive values above the origin and negative values below the origin. Any point on the plane can be found with an ordered pair.

This ordered pair comes in the form of $(x,y)$. This pair is known as coordinates. The $x$-value of the coordinate is called the abscissa. The $y$-value of the coordinate is called the ordinate. The two number lines divide the plane into four parts. Each part is known as a quadrant. The quadrants are labeled as I, II, III, and IV.

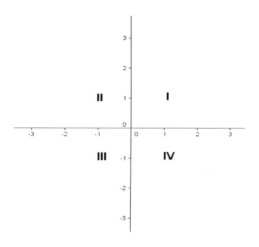

Example 1
The following points go on the coordinate plane:
A. $(-4, -2)$ | B. $(-1, 3)$ | C. $(2, 2)$ | D. $(3, -1)$

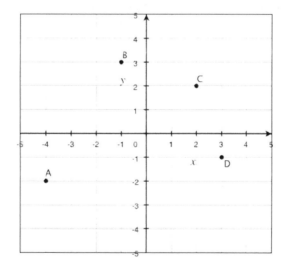

Before learning the different forms of equations for graphing, you need to know some definitions. A ratio of the change in the vertical distance to the change in horizontal distance is called the *Slope*.

On a graph with two points, $(x_1, y_1)$ and $(x_2, y_2)$, the slope is found with the formula $= \frac{y_2 - y_1}{x_2 - x_1}$; where $x_1 \neq x_2$ and m stands for slope. If the value of the slope is positive, the line has an upward direction from left to right. If the value of the slope is negative, the line has a downward direction from left to right. The example of the graph below is a positive slope.

If the $y$-coordinates are the same for both points, the slope is zero. So, the line is a *Horizontal Line*. If the $x$-coordinates are the same for both points, there is no slope. So, the line is a

*Vertical Line.* Two or more lines that have equal slopes are *Parallel Lines. Perpendicular Lines* have slopes that are negative reciprocals of each other. For example, $\frac{a}{b}$ and $\frac{-b}{a}$.

Example
With the graph below, write an equation in slope-intercept form that describes the line.

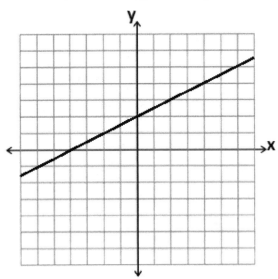

First, find several coordinates on the graph. Then, put them into a table:

| x | y |
|----|----|
| -6 | -1 |
| -4 | 0 |
| -2 | 1 |
| 0 | 2 |
| 2 | 3 |

Next, find a relationship between *x* and *y*. In this case, as *x* increases by 2, *y* increases by 1. This means that *m* = 0.5. The reason is that *y* changes by half the amount that *x* does. Also, you know that *b* = 2. The reason is that the graph crosses the y-axis at 2. So, the equation for this graph is $y = 0.5x + 2$.

This is a list of some forms of equations:
- *Standard Form: Ax + By = C*; the slope is $\frac{-A}{B}$ and the *y*-intercept is $\frac{C}{B}$
- *Slope Intercept Form:* $y = mx + b$, where *m* is the slope and *b* is the *y*-intercept
- *Point-Slope Form:* $y - y_1 = m(x - x_1)$, where *m* is the slope and $(x_1, y_1)$ is a point on the line
- *Two-Point Form:* $\frac{y-y_1}{x-x_1} = \frac{y_2-y_1}{x_2-x_1}$, where $(x_1, y_1)$ and $(x_2, y_2)$ are two points on the given line
- *Intercept Form:* $\frac{x}{x_1} + \frac{y}{y_1} = 1$, where $(x_1, 0)$ is the point at which a line intersects the *x*-axis, and $(0, y_1)$ is the point at which the same line intersects the *y*-axis

## Unit Rate as the Slope

A new book goes on sale in book stores and online stores. In the first month, 5,000 copies of the book are sold. Over time, the book continues to grow in popularity. The data for the number of copies sold is in the table below.

| # of Months on Sale | 1 | 2 | 3 | 4 | 5 |
|---|---|---|---|---|---|
| # of Copies Sold (In Thousands) | 5 | 10 | 15 | 20 | 25 |

So, the number of copies that are sold and the time that the book is on sale is a proportional relationship. In this example, an equation can be used to show the data: y=5x, where x is the number of months that the book is on sale. Also, y is the number of copies sold. So, the slope is $\frac{rise}{run} = \frac{5}{1}$. This can be reduced to 5.

## Calculations Using Points

Sometimes you need to do calculations by using points on a graph. With these points, you can find the midpoint and distance. If you know the equation for a line you can find the distance between the line and the point.

To find the *Midpoint* of two points $(x_1, y_1)$ and $(x_2, y_2)$, you need the average of the x-coordinates. This average will give you the x-coordinate of the midpoint. Then, take the average of the y-coordinates. This will give you the y-coordinate of the midpoint. The formula is $\left(\frac{x_1+x_2}{2}, \frac{y_1+y_2}{2}\right)$ = midpoint.

The *Distance* between two points is the same as the length of the hypotenuse of a right triangle. So, there is the length of the segment that is parallel to the x-axis. This segment is the difference between the x-coordinates of the two points. Also, there is the length of the segment parallel to the y-axis. This is the difference between the y-coordinates of the two points. Use the Pythagorean Theorem $a^2 + b^2 = c^2$ or $c = \sqrt{a^2 + b^2}$ to find the distance. The formula is $\sqrt{(x_2 - x_1)^2 + (y_2 - y_1)^2}$ = distance.

A line may be given as $Ax + By + C = 0$ where $A$, $B$, and $C$ are coefficients. With this equation, you can use a point $(x_1, y_1)$ not on the line and use the formula $d = \frac{|Ax_1 + By_1 + C|}{\sqrt{A^2 + B^2}}$. This formula will give the distance between the line and the point $(x_1, y_1)$.

> ➤ **Review Video: <u>Distance & Midpoint Formulas</u>**
> *Visit **mometrix.com/academy** and enter **Code: 973653***

## Transformation

- Rotation: An object is rotated, or turned, between 0 and 360 degrees, around a fixed point. The size and shape of the object are unchanged.
- Reflection: An object is reflected, or flipped, across a line, so that the original object and reflected object are the same distance from the line of reflection. The size and shape of the object are unchanged.
- Translation: An object is translated, or shifted, horizontally and/or vertically to a new location. The orientation, size, and shape of the object are unchanged.

Rotation

*A line segment begins at (1, 4) and ends at (5, 4). Draw the line segment and rotate the line segment 90º about the point (3, 4).*

The point about which the line segment is being rotated is on the line segment. This point should be on both the original and rotated line. The point (3, 4) is the center of the original line segment, and should still be the center of the rotated line segment. The dashed line is the rotated line segment.

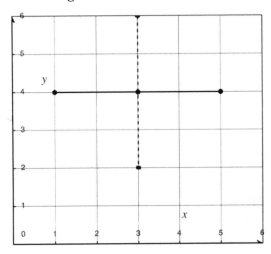

Reflection

*Example 1*: To create a congruent rectangle by reflecting, first draw a line of reflection. The line can be next to or on the figure. Then draw the image reflected across this line.

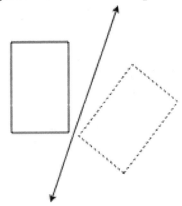

*Example 2*: A line segment begins at (1, 5) and ends at (5, 4). Draw the line segment, then reflect the line segment across the line $y = 3$.

To reflect a segment, consider folding a piece of paper at the line of reflection. The new image should line up exactly with the old image when the paper is folded. The dashed line is the reflected line segment.

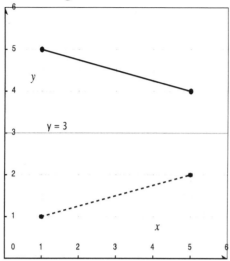

## Translation

*Example 1:* A line segment on an x-y grid starts at (3, 2) and ends at (4, 1). Draw the line segment, and translate the segment up 2 units and left 2 units.

The solid line segment is the original line segment, and the dashed line is the translated line segment. The *y*-coordinate of each point has increased by 2, because the points moved two units away from 0. The *x*-coordinate of each point has decreased by 2, because the points moved two units closer to 0.

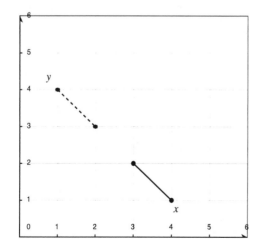

*Example 2:* Identify a transformation that could have been performed on the solid triangle to result in the dashed triangle.

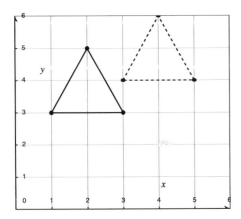

The transformed triangle has the same orientation as the original triangle. It has been shifted up one unit and two units to the right. Because the orientation of the figure has not changed, and its new position can be described using shifts up and to the right, the figure was translated.

## Angles

An angle is made when two lines or line segments meet at a point. The angle may be a starting point for a pair of segments or rays. Also, angles come from the intersection of lines. The symbol ∠ stands for angles. Angles that are opposite to one another are called vertical angles, and their measures are equal. The vertex is the point where two segments or rays meet to make an angle. Angles that are made from intersecting rays, lines, and/or line segments have four angles at the vertex.

An acute angle is an angle with a degree measure less than 90°. A right angle is an angle with a degree measure of exactly 90°. An obtuse angle is an angle with a degree measure greater than 90° but less than 180°. A straight angle is an angle with a degree measure of exactly 180°. A reflex angle is an angle with a degree measure greater than 180° but less than 360°. A full angle is an angle with a degree measure of exactly 360°.

> ➤ **Review Video: Angles**
> *Visit **mometrix.com/academy** and enter **Code: 264624***

Two angles with a sum of exactly 90° are known as complementary. The two angles may or may not be adjacent (i.e., *next to* or *beside*). In a right triangle, the two acute angles are complementary.

Two angles with a sum that is exactly 180° are known as supplementary. The two angles may or may not be adjacent. Two intersecting lines always make two pairs of supplementary angles. Adjacent supplementary angles will always make a straight line.

## Triangles

An equilateral triangle is a triangle with three congruent sides. Also, an equilateral triangle will have three congruent angles and each angle will be 60°. All equilateral triangles are acute triangles.

An isosceles triangle is a triangle with two congruent sides. An isosceles triangle will have two congruent angles as well.

A scalene triangle is a triangle with no congruent sides. Also, a scalene triangle will have three angles of different measures. The angle with the largest measure is opposite from the longest side. The angle with the smallest measure is opposite from the shortest side.

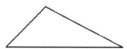

An acute triangle is a triangle whose three angles are all less than 90°. If two of the angles are equal, the acute triangle is also an isosceles triangle. If the three angles are all equal, the acute triangle is also an equilateral triangle.

A right triangle is a triangle with exactly one angle equal to 90°. A right triangle can never be acute or obtuse.

An obtuse triangle is a triangle with one angle greater than 90°. The other two angles may or may not be equal. If the two remaining angles are equal, the obtuse triangle is also an isosceles triangle.

## Congruency, Similarity, and Symmetry

Congruent figures are geometric figures that have the same size and shape. All corresponding angles are equal, and all corresponding sides are equal. Congruence is shown by the symbol ≅.

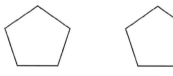

Congruent polygons

Similar figures are geometric figures that have the same shape, but may not have the same size. All corresponding angles are equal, and all corresponding sides are proportional. However, they do not have to be equal. Similarity is shown by the symbol ~.

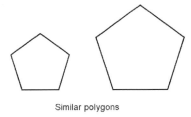

Similar polygons

Note that all congruent figures are also similar. However, not all similar figures are congruent.

Line of Symmetry: The line that divides a figure or object into equal parts. Each part is congruent to the other. An object may have no lines of symmetry, one line of symmetry, or multiple (i.e., more than one) lines of symmetry.

Lines of symmetry:

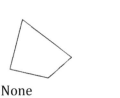
None

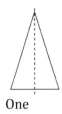
One

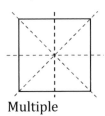
Multiple

**Polygons**

Each straight line segment of a polygon is called a side. The point at which two sides of a polygon intersect is called the vertex. In a polygon, the number of sides is always equal to the number of vertices. A polygon with all sides congruent and all angles equal is called a regular polygon.

A line segment from the center of a polygon that is perpendicular to a side of the polygon is called the apothem. A line segment from the center of a polygon to a vertex of the polygon is called a radius. In a regular polygon, the apothem can be used to find the area of the polygon using the formula $A = \frac{1}{2}ap$, where $a$ is the apothem, and $p$ is the perimeter.

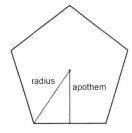

Triangle – 3 sides
Quadrilateral – 4 sides
Pentagon – 5 sides
Hexagon – 6 sides
Heptagon – 7 sides
Octagon – 8 sides
Nonagon – 9 sides
Decagon – 10 sides
Dodecagon – 12 sides

Generally, an *n*-gon is a polygon that has more than 12 angles and sides. The space of *n* is for the number of sides. Also, an 11-sided polygon is known as an 11-gon.

Quadrilateral: A closed two-dimensional geometric figure that has four straight sides. The sum of the interior angles of any quadrilateral is 360°. A quadrilateral whose diagonals divide each other is a parallelogram.

A quadrilateral whose opposite sides are parallel (i.e., 2 pairs of parallel sides) is a parallelogram. A quadrilateral whose diagonals are perpendicular bisectors of each other is a rhombus. A quadrilateral with opposite sides (i.e., both pairs) that are parallel and congruent is a rhombus.

Parallelogram: A quadrilateral that has two pairs of opposite parallel sides. The sides that are parallel are also congruent. The opposite interior angles are always congruent, and the consecutive interior angles are supplementary. The diagonals of a parallelogram divide each other. Each diagonal divides the parallelogram into two congruent triangles.

A parallelogram that has a right angle is a rectangle. In the diagram below, the top left corner and the bottom left corner are consecutive angles. Consecutive angles of a parallelogram are supplementary. If there is one right angle in a parallelogram, there are four right angles in that parallelogram.

Trapezoid: Normally, a quadrilateral has one pair of parallel sides. Some define a trapezoid as a quadrilateral that has at least one pair of parallel sides. There are no rules for the second pair of sides. So, there are no rules for the diagonals of a trapezoid.

Rectangles, rhombuses, and squares are all special forms of parallelograms.

Rectangle: A parallelogram with four right angles. All rectangles are parallelograms, but not all parallelograms are rectangles. The diagonals of a rectangle are congruent.

Rhombus: A parallelogram with four congruent sides. All rhombuses are parallelograms, but not all parallelograms are rhombuses. The diagonals of a rhombus are perpendicular to each other.

A rhombus with one right angle is a square. The rhombus is a special form of a parallelogram. So, the rules about the angles of a parallelogram are true for the rhombus.

Square: A parallelogram with four right angles and four congruent sides. All squares are also parallelograms, rhombuses, and rectangles. The diagonals of a square are congruent and perpendicular to each other.

**Three Dimensional Figures**

Right Rectangular Prism
A rectangular prism has six rectangular faces. The six faces give it 12 edges and eight vertices.

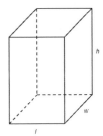

## Cube
A cube has six square faces. The six faces give it 12 edges and eight vertices.

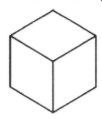

## Sphere
A sphere is a perfectly round object that has no faces, edges, or vertices. This three-dimensional object is similar to the two-dimensional circle.

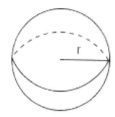

## Right Triangular Prism
A triangular prism has five faces. Two faces are triangles, and three faces are rectangles. This prism has 9 edges and six vertices.

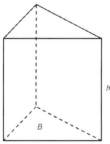

## Cylinder
The cylinder has two circular faces. In three dimensions, the cylinder has edges or vertices.

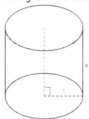

## Right Rectangular Pyramid

A rectangular pyramid has four triangular faces and one rectangular face. This pyramid has eight edges and five vertices.

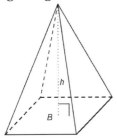

## Cone

A cone has one circular face. Cones do not have any edges or vertices. The cones that you will encounter are right circular. This means that they have a circle for a base instead of a polygonal base. A pyramid is a cone with a polygonal base.

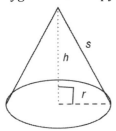

# Measurement

## Area and Perimeter Formulas

The perimeter of any triangle is found by adding the three side lengths $P = a + b + c$. For an equilateral triangle, this is the same as $P = 3s$, where $s$ is any side length. The reason is that the three sides are the same length.

*Find the side of a triangle*
You may have problems that give you the perimeter of a triangle. So, you are asked to find one of the sides.
Example: The perimeter of a triangle is 35 cm. One side length is 10 cm. Another side length is 20cm. Find the length of the missing side.

      First:   Set up the equation to set apart a side length.
              Now, the equation is $35 = 10 + 20 + c$. So, you are left with $35 = 30 + c$.

      Second: Subtract 30 from both sides: $35 - 30 = 30 - 30 + c$
              Then, you are left with $5 = c$

The area of any triangle can be found by taking half of the base (i.e., $b$). Then, multiply that result by the height (i.e., $h$) of the triangle. So, the standard formula for the area of a triangle is $A = \frac{1}{2}bh$. For many triangles, it may be difficult to calculate $h$. So, other formulas are given here that may be easier.

*Find the height or the area of the base*
You may have problems that give you the area of a triangle. So, you are asked to find the height or the base.
Example: The area of a triangle is 70 cm², and the height is 10. Find the base.

First: Set up the equation to set apart the base.

The equation is $70 = \frac{1}{2}10b$.

Now, multiply both sides by 2: $70 \times 2 = \frac{1}{2}10b \times 2$.

So, you are left with: $140 = 10b$.

Second: Divide both sides by 10 to get the base: $\frac{140}{10} = \frac{10b}{10}$

Then, you have $14 = b$.

Note: When you need to find the height, you can follow the steps above to find it.

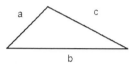

➢ **Review Video: <u>Area and Perimeter of a Triangle</u>**
*Visit **mometrix.com/academy** and enter **Code: 817385***

Another formula that works for any triangle is $A = \sqrt{s(s-a)(s-b)(s-c)}$, where $A$ is the area, $s$ is the semi-perimeter $s = \frac{a+b+c}{2}$, and $a$, $b$, and $c$ are the lengths of the three sides. The area of an equilateral triangle can found by the formula $A = \frac{\sqrt{3}}{4}s^2$, where $A$ is the area and $s$ is the length of a side. You could use the $30° - 60° - 90°$ ratios to find the height of the triangle. Then, use the standard triangle area formula.

The area of an isosceles triangle can found by the formula, $A = \frac{1}{2}b\sqrt{a^2 - \frac{b^2}{4}}$, where $A$ is the area, $b$ is the base, and $a$ is the length of one of the two congruent sides. If you do not remember this formula, you can use the Pythagorean Theorem to find the height. Then, you can use the standard formula for the area of a triangle.

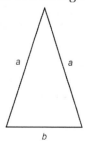

The area of a square is found by using the formula $A = s^2$, where $A$ is the area and $s$ is the length of one side.

*Find the side of a square*
You may have problems that give you the area of a square. So, you are asked to find the side.
Example: The area of a square is 9 cm². Find the side.

First:   Set up the equation to set apart $s$.
The equation is $9 = s^2$.

Second: Now, you can take the square root of both sides: $\sqrt{9} = \sqrt{s^2}$.
So, you are left with: $3 = s$

The perimeter of a square is found by using the formula $P = 4s$, where P is the perimeter, and $s$ is the length of one side. All four sides are equal in a square. So, you can multiply the length of one side by 4. This is faster than adding the same number four times.

*Find the side of a square*
You may have problems that give you the perimeter of a square. So, you are asked to find the side.
Example: The perimeter of a square is 60 cm. Find the side.

First:   Set up the equation to set apart $s$.
The equation is $60 = 4s$.

Second: Now, you can divide both sides by 4: $\frac{60}{4} = \frac{4s}{4}$. You are left with $15 = s$

> ➢ **Review Video: <u>Area and Perimeter of a Square</u>**
> *Visit **mometrix.com/academy** and enter **Code: 620902***

The area of a rectangle is found by the formula $A = lw$, where $A$ is the area of the rectangle, $l$ is the length and $w$ is the width. Usually, the longer side is the length, and the shorter side is the width. However, the numbers for $l$ and $w$ can used be for one or the other.

*Find the width or length of a rectangle*
You may have problems that give you the area of a rectangle. So, you are asked to find the width.
Example: The area of a rectangle is 150cm², and the length is 10cm. Find the width.

First:   Set up the equation to set apart width.
The equation is $150 = 10w$.

Second: Divide both sides by 10: $\frac{150}{10} = \frac{10w}{10}$. You are left with $15 = w$

Note: When you need to find the length, you can follow the steps above to find it.

The perimeter of a rectangle can be found with two formulas $P = 2l + 2w$ or $P = 2(l + w)$, where $l$ is the length, and $w$ is the width.

*Find the width or length of a rectangle*
You may have problems that give you the perimeter of a rectangle. So, you are asked to find the width.

Example: The perimeter of a rectangle is 100cm, and the length is 20cm. Find the width.

First:   Set up the equation to set apart the width.
The equation is $100 = 2(20 + w)$

Second: Distribute the 2 across $(20 + w)$: $100 = 40 + 2w$

Then, subtract 40 from both sides: $100 - 40 = 40 + 2w - 40$

So, you are left with: $60 = 2w$. Then, divide both sides by 2: $\frac{60}{2} = \frac{2w}{2}$.

Now, you have $30 = w$.

Note: When you need to find the length, you can follow the steps above to find it.

> **Review Video: <u>Area and Perimeter of a Rectangle</u>**
> *Visit **mometrix.com/academy** and enter **Code: 933707***

The area of a parallelogram is found by the formula $A = bh$, where $b$ is the length of the base, and $h$ is the height. Note that the base and height match with the length and width in a rectangle. So, this formula can be used for rectangles as well. Do not confuse the height of a parallelogram with the length of the second side. They have the same measure only with rectangles.

*Find the length of the base or the height of a parallelogram*
You may have problems that give you the area of a parallelogram. So, you are asked to find the area of the base or the height.
Example: The area of the parallelogram is 84 cm². The base is 7cm. Find the height.

Set up the equation to set apart the height.

So, you have $84 = 7h$. Now, divide both sides by 7: $\frac{84}{7} = \frac{7h}{7}$.

Then, you are left with $12 = h$

The perimeter of a parallelogram is found by the formula $P = 2a + 2b$ or $P = 2(a + b)$, where $a$ and $b$ are the lengths of the two sides.

*Find the missing side of a parallelogram*
You may have problems that give you the perimeter of a parallelogram. So, you are asked to find one of the sides. Example: The perimeter of a parallelogram is 100cm, and one side is 20cm. Find the other side.

First:   Set up the equation to set apart one of the side lengths.

The equation is $100 = 2(20 + b)$

Second: Distribute the 2 across $(20 + b)$: $100 = 40 + 2b$

Then, subtract 40 from both sides: $100 - 40 = 40 + 2b - 40$

So, you are left with: $60 = 2b$. Then, divide both sides by 2: $\frac{60}{2} = \frac{2b}{2}$

Now, you have $30 = b$.

> **Review Video: <u>Area and Perimeter of a Parallelogram</u>**
> *Visit **mometrix.com/academy** and enter **Code: 718313***

The area of a trapezoid is found by the formula $A = \frac{1}{2}h(b_1 + b_2)$, where $h$ is the height, and $b_1$ and $b_2$ are the two parallel sides (i.e., bases). The height is the segment that joins the parallel bases.

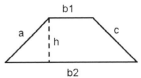

*Find the height of a trapezoid*
You may have problems that give you the area of a trapezoid. So, you are asked to find the height.
Example: The area of a trapezoid is 30cm². $B_1$ is 3cm, and $B_2$ is 9cm. Find the height.

First: Set up the equation to set apart the height.
The equation is $30 = \frac{1}{2}h(3 + 9)$.

Second: Now, multiply both sides by 2: $30 \times 2 = \frac{1}{2}(12)h \times 2$.
So, you are left with: $60 = (12)h$.

Third: Divide both sides by 12: $\frac{60}{12} = \frac{(12)h}{12}$. Now, you have $5 = h$

*Find a base of a trapezoid*
You may have problems that give you the area of a trapezoid and the height. So, you are asked to find one of the bases.
Example: The area of a trapezoid is 90cm². $b_1$ is 5cm, and the height is 12cm. Find $b_2$.

First: Set up the equation to set apart $b_2$.
The equation is $90 = \frac{1}{2}12(5 + b_2)$.

Second: Now, multiply the height by $\frac{1}{2}$: $90 = 6(5 + b_2)$.
So, you can distribute the 6 across $(5 + b_2)$: $90 = 30 + 6b_2$

Third: Subtract 30 from both sides $90 - 30 = 30 + 6b_2 - 30$.
Now, you have $60 = 6b_2$.
Then, divide both sides by 6: $\frac{60}{6} = \frac{6b_2}{6}$. So, $b_2 = 10$.

The perimeter of a trapezoid is found by the formula $P = a + b_1 + c + b_2$, where $a, b_1, c,$ and $b_2$ are the four sides of the trapezoid.

*Find the missing side of a trapezoid*
Example: The perimeter of a trapezoid is 50cm. $B_1$ is 20cm, $B_2$ is 10cm, and a is 5cm. Find the length of side c.

First: Set up the equation to set apart the missing side.
The equation is $50 = 5 + 20 + c + 10$. So, you have $50 = 35 + c$

Second: Subtract 35 from both sides: $50 - 35 = 35 + c - 35$.
So, you are left with $15 = c$

> **Review Video: <u>Area and Perimeter of a Trapezoid</u>**
> *Visit **mometrix.com/academy** and enter **Code: 587523***

## Circles

The center is the single point inside the circle that is equidistant from every point on the circle. The point $O$ is in the diagram below. The radius is a line segment that joins the center of the circle and any one point on the circle. All radii of a circle are equal. The segments $OX$, $OY$, and $OZ$ are in the diagram below. The diameter is a line segment that passes through the center of the circle and has both endpoints inside the circle. The length of the diameter is twice the length of the radius. The segment $XZ$ is in the diagram below. Concentric circles are circles that have the same center but not the same length of radii. A bulls-eye target is an example of concentric circles.

The **area of a circle** is found with the formula $A = \pi r^2$, where $r$ is the length of the radius. If the diameter of the circle is given, divide it in half to get the radius before using the formula. (Note: In the following formulas, 3.14 is used for $\pi$.)

The **circumference of a circle** is found by the formula $C = 2\pi r$, where $r$ is the radius.

> ➤ **Review Video: <u>Area and Circumference of a Circle</u>**
> *Visit **mometrix.com/academy** and enter **Code: 243015***

## Surface Area and Volume Formulas

<u>Prism</u>

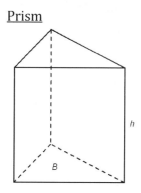

The **volume of any prism** is found with the formula $V = Bh$, where $B$ is the area of the base, and $h$ is the height. The perpendicular distance between the bases is the height.

*Find the area of the base or the height of a prism*
You may have problems that give you the volume of a prism. So, you are asked to find the area of the base or the height.
Example: The volume of the prism is 200 cm³. The area of the base is 10cm. Find the height.
      First:   Set up the equation to set apart the height.
            So, you have $200 = 10h$.

Second: Now, divide both sides by 10: $\frac{200}{10} = \frac{10h}{10}$.
Then, you are left with $20 = h$

Note: When you need to find the area of the base, you can follow the steps above to solve for it.

The **surface area of any prism** is the sum of the areas of both bases and all sides. So, the formula for a sphere is $SA = 2B + Ph$, where $B$ is the area of the base, $P$ is the perimeter of the base, and $h$ is the height of the prism.

*Find the area of the base*
You may have problems that give you the surface area of a prism. So, you are asked to find the area of the base.
Example: The surface area of the prism is 100 cm². The perimeter of the base is 10cm, and the height is 2cm. Find the area of the base.
    First:   Set up the equation to set apart the area of the base.
            So, you have $100 = 2B + 20$.

    Second: Subtract 20 from both sides: $100 - 20 = 2B + 20 - 20$.
            Now, you are left with $80 = 2B$. So, divide both sides by 2.
            Then, you have $40 = B$.

*Find the perimeter of the base or the height of a prism*
You may have problems that give you the surface area of a prism and the area of the base. So, you are asked to find the perimeter of the base or the height.
Example: The surface area of the prism is 280 cm². The area of the base is 15cm², and the perimeter of the base is 10cm. Find the height.
    First:   Set up the equation to set apart the height.
            The equation is $280 = 2(15) + (10)h$. So, you have $250 = 30 + (10)h$

    Second: Subtract 30 from both sides: $280 - 30 = 30 + (10)h - 30$.
            Now, you are left with: $250 = (10)h$.
            Then, divide both sides by 10.
            $\frac{250}{10} = \frac{(10)h}{10} = 25$. So, the height of the prism is 25cm.

Note: When you need to find the perimeter of the base, you can follow the steps above to find it.

Rectangular Prism

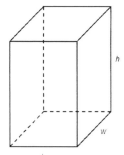

The **volume of a rectangular prism** can be found with the formula $V = lwh$, where $V$ is the volume, $l$ is the length, $w$ is the width, and $h$ is the height.

*Find the length, width, or height of a rectangular prism*
You may have problems that give you the volume of a rectangular prism. So, you are asked to find the length, width, or height.
Example: The volume of the rectangular prism is 200 cm³. The width is 10cm, and the height is 10cm. Find the length.
    First:    Set up the equation to set apart the length.
            So, you have $200 = l(10)(10)$ that becomes $200 = (100)l$.

    Second: Divide both sides by 100.
            Now, you have $\frac{200}{100} = \frac{(100)l}{100}$. So, you are left with $2 = l$.

Note: When you need to find the width or height, you can follow the steps above to solve for either.

The **surface area of a rectangular prism** can be calculated as $SA = 2lw + 2hl + 2wh$ or $SA = 2(lw + hl + wh)$.

*Find the length, width, or height of a rectangular prism*
You may have problems that give you the surface area of a rectangular prism. So, you are asked to find the length, width, or height.
Example: The surface area of the rectangular prism is 200 cm². The width is 15cm, and the height is 5cm. Find the length.
    First:    Set up the equation to set apart the length.
            So, you have $200 = 2(15)l + 2(5)l + 2(15)(5)$ that becomes $200 = (40)l + 150$.

    Second: Subtract 150 from both sides.
            So, $200 - 150 = (40)l + 150 - 150$ becomes $50 = (40)l$.
            Then, divide both sides by 40 to set apart $l$: $\frac{50}{40} = \frac{(40)l}{40}$.
            You are left with $1.25 = l$.

Note: When you need to find the width or height, you can follow the steps above to solve for either.

    &#10148;  **Review Video: <u>Volume and Surface Area of a Rectangular Solid</u>**
        *Visit **mometrix.com/academy** and enter **Code: 386780***

## Cube

The **volume of a cube** can be found with the formula $V = s^3$, where $s$ is the length of a side.

The **surface area of a cube** is calculated as $SA = 6s^2$, where $SA$ is the total surface area and $s$ is the length of a side. These formulas are the same as the ones used for the volume and surface area of a rectangular prism. However, these are simple formulas because the three numbers (i.e., length, width, and height) are the same.

## Conversion

When going from a larger unit to a smaller unit, multiply the number of the known amount by the equivalent amount. When going from a smaller unit to a larger unit, divide the number of the known amount by the equivalent amount.

Also, you can set up conversion fractions. In these fractions, one fraction is the conversion factor. The other fraction has the unknown amount in the numerator. So, the known value is placed in the denominator. Sometimes the second fraction has the known value from the problem in the numerator, and the unknown in the denominator. Multiply the two fractions to get the converted measurement.

Measurement Equivalents
*Inches, Yards, and Feet*
12 inches = 1 foot
1 yard = 3 feet
1 yard = 36 inches

*1 mile in feet and yards*
1 mile = 5280 feet
1 mile = 1760 yards

*1 quart in pints and cups*
1 quart = 2 pints
1 quart = 4 cups

*1 gallon in quarts, pints, and cups*
1 gallon = 4 quarts
1 gallon = 8 pints
1 gallon = 16 cups

*1 pound in ounces*
1 pound = 16 ounces

Don't think that because something weighs one pound that its volume is one pint. Ounces of weight are not equal to fluid ounces which measure volume.

*1 ton in pounds*
1 ton = 2000 pounds

Metric measurements
*1 liter in milliliters and cubic centimeters*
1 liter = 1000 milliliters
1 liter = 1000 cubic centimeters

Do not confuse *cubic centimeters* with *centiliters*. 1 liter = 1000 cubic centi*meters*, but 1 liter = 100 centi*liters*.

*1 meter in millimeters and centimeters*
1 meter = 1000 millimeters
1 meter = 100 centimeters

*1 gram in milligrams*
1 gram = 1000 milligrams

*1 kilogram in grams*
1 kilogram = 1000 grams

Kilo, centi, and milli
Kilo-: one thousand
Centi-: one hundredth
Milli-: one thousandth

*Example 1*
There are 100 centimeters in 1 meter. Convert the measurements below.
a. Convert 1.4 m to cm
b. Convert 218 cm to m

Write a ratio with the conversion factor: $\frac{100 \text{ cm}}{1 \text{ m}}$. Use proportions to convert the given units.

a. $\frac{100 \text{ cm}}{1 \text{ m}} = \frac{x \text{ cm}}{1.4 \text{ m}}$. Cross multiply to get $x = 140$. So, there are 1.4 m in 140 cm.

b. $\frac{100 \text{ cm}}{1 \text{ m}} = \frac{218 \text{ cm}}{x \text{ m}}$. Cross multiply to get $100x = 218$, or $x = 2.18$. So, there are 218 cm in 2.18 m.

*Example 2*
There are 12 inches in 1 foot. Also, there are 3 feet in 1 yard. Convert the following measurements.
a. 42 inches to feet
b. 15 feet to yards

Write ratios with the conversion factors: $\frac{12 \text{ in}}{1 \text{ ft}}$ and: $\frac{3 \text{ ft}}{1 \text{ yd}}$. Use proportions to convert the given units.

a. $\frac{12 \text{ in}}{1 \text{ ft}} = \frac{42 \text{ in}}{x \text{ ft}}$. Cross multiply to get $12x = 42$, or $x = 3.5$. So, there are 42 inches in 3.5 feet.

b. $\frac{3 \text{ ft}}{1 \text{ yd}} = \frac{15 \text{ ft}}{x \text{ yd}}$. Cross multiply to get $3x = 15$, or $x = 5$. So, there are 15 feet in 5 yards.

# Data Analysis and Probability

## Measures of Central Tendency

The quantities of mean, median, and mode are known as measures of central tendency. Each can give a picture of what a whole set of data looks like with a single number. Knowing what each value stands for is important to understanding the information from these measures.

### Mean

The mean, or the arithmetic mean or average, of a data set is found by adding all of the values in the set. Then you divide the sum by how many values that you had in a set. For example, a data set has 6 numbers, and the sum of those 6 numbers is 30. So, the mean is $30/6 = 5$. When you know the average, you may be asked to find a missing value. Look over the following steps for how this is done.

Example: You are given the values of 5, 10, 12, and 13. Also, you are told that the average is 9.6. So, what is the one missing value?

First: Add the known values together: $5 + 10 + 12 + 13 = 40$.
Now, set up an equation with the sum of the known values in the divisor. Then, put the number of values in the dividend. For this example, you have 5 values. So, you have $\frac{40+?}{5} = 9.6$. Now, multiply both sides by 5: $5 \times \frac{40+?}{5} = 9.6 \times 5$

Second: You are left with $40+? = 48$. Now, subtract 40 from both sides: $40 - 40 + ? = 48 - 40$. So, you know that the missing value is 8.

### Median

The median is the middle value of a data set. The median can be found by putting the data set in numerical order (e.g., 3, 7, 26, 28, 39). Then, you pick the value that is in the middle of the set. In the data set (1, 2, 3, 4, 5), there is an odd number of values. So, the median is 3. Sometimes, there is an even number of values in the set. So, the median can be found by taking the average of the two middle values. In the data set (1, 2, 3, 4, 5, 6), the median would be $(3 + 4)/2 = 3.5$.

### Mode

The mode is the value that appears the most in a data set. In the data set (1, 2, 3, 4, 5, 5, 5), the number 5 appears more than the other numbers. So, the value 5 is the mode. If more than one value appears the same number of times, then there are multiple values for the mode. For example, a data set is (1, 2, 2, 3, 4, 4, 5, 5). So, the modes would be 2, 4, and 5. Now, if no value appears more than any other value in the data set, then there is no mode.

> ➤ **Review Video: <u>Mean, Median, and Mode</u>**
> *Visit **mometrix.com/academy** and enter **Code: 286207***

### Range

The range is the difference between the greatest data point and the least data point in the set. In the set (12, 23, 1, 8, 45, 22), the greatest data point is 45. The least data point is 1. When you subtract 1 from 45, you have 44. So, 44 is the range of the data set.

**First and Third Quartile**

First Quartile
The first quartile of a data set is the median of the front half of a data set. A simple way to find this is to set up the first quartile as the first half of the ordered data and find the median. Do not include the median of the full data set if there are an odd number of data points.
For example, you have the data set {3, 1, 12, 7, 17, 4, 10, 8, 9, 20, 4}. Put the data in order to get {1, 3, 4, 4, 7, 8, 9, 10, 12, 17, 20}. The front half that does not include the median of eight is {1, 3, 4, 4, 7}. This has a median of 4. So, the first quartile of this data set is 4.

Third Quartile
The third quartile of a data set is the median of the back half of a data set. A simple way to find this is to set up the third quartile as the back half of the ordered data and find the median. Do not include the median of the full data set if there are an odd number of data points.
For example, you have the data set {3, 1, 12, 7, 17, 4, 10, 8, 9, 20, 4}. Put the data in order to get {1, 3, 4, 4, 7, 8, 9, 10, 12, 17, 20}. The back half that does not include the median of eight is {9, 10, 12, 17, 20}. This has a median of 12. So, the third quartile of this data set is 12.

**Common Charts and Graphs**

*Charts* and *Tables* are ways of organizing information into separate rows and columns. These rows and columns are labeled to find and to explain the information in them. Some charts and tables are organized horizontally with rows giving the details about the labeled information. Other charts and tables are organized vertically with columns giving the details about the labeled information.

A *Bar Graph* is one of the few graphs that can be drawn correctly in two ways: horizontally and vertically. A bar graph is similar to a line plot because of how the data is organized on the graph. Both axes must have their categories defined for the graph to be useful. A thick line is drawn from zero to the exact value of the data. This line can be used for a number, a percentage, or other numerical value. Longer bar lengths point to greater data values. To understand a bar graph, read the labels for the axes to know the units being reported. Then look where the bars end and match this to the scale on the other axis. This will show you the connection between the axes. This bar graph shows the responses from a survey about the favorite colors of a group.

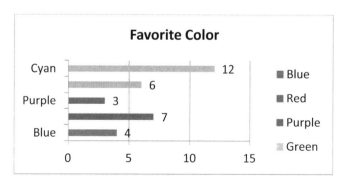

*Line Graphs* have one or more lines of different styles (e.g., solid or broken). These lines show the different values for a data set. Each point on the graph is shown as an ordered pair. This is similar to a Cartesian plane. In this case, the *x*- and *y*- axes are given certain units (e.g., dollars or time). Each point that is for one measurement is joined by line segments. Then, these lines show what the values are doing. The lines may be increasing (i.e., line sloping upward), decreasing (i.e., line sloping downward), or staying the same (i.e., horizontal line). More than one set of data can be put on the same line graph. This is done to compare more than one piece of data. An example of this would be graphing test scores for different groups of students over the same stretch of time. This allows you to see which group had the greatest increase or decrease in performance over a certain amount of years. This example is shown in the graph below.

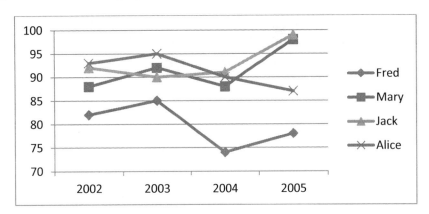

A *Line Plot*, or a *Dot Plot*, has plotted points that are NOT connected by line segments. In this graph, the horizontal axis lists the different possible values for the data. The vertical axis lists how many times one value happens. A single dot is graphed for each value. The dots in a line plot are connected. If the dots are connected, then this will not correctly represent the data.

A *Pictograph* is a graph that is given in the horizontal format. This graph uses pictures or symbols to show the data. Each pictograph must have a key that defines the picture or symbol. Also, this key should give the number that stands for each picture or symbol. The pictures or symbols on a pictograph are not always shown as whole elements.

In this case, the fraction of the picture or symbol stands for the same fraction of the quantity that a whole picture or symbol represents. For example, there is a row in the pictograph with $3\frac{1}{2}$ ears of corn. Each ear of corn represents 100 stalks of corn in a field. So, this would equal $3\frac{1}{2} \times 100 = 350$ stalks of corn in the field.

*Circle Graphs*, or *Pie Charts*, show the relationship of each type of data compared to the whole set of data. The circle graph is divided into sections by drawing radii (i.e., plural for radius) to make central angles. These angles stand for a percentage of the circle. Each 1% of data is equal to 3.6° in the graph. So, data that stands for a 90° section of the circle graph makes up 25% of the whole. The pie chart below shows the data from the frequency table where people were asked about their favorite color.

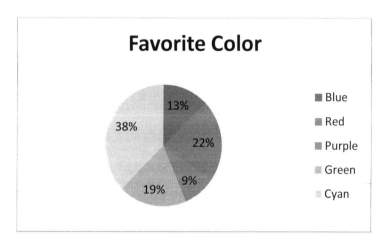

**Probability**

Probability is a branch of statistics that deals with the likelihood of something taking place. One classic example is a coin toss. There are only two possible results: heads or tails. The likelihood, or probability, that the coin will land as heads is 1 out of 2 (i.e., 1/2, 0.5, 50%). Tails has the same probability. Another common example is a 6-sided die roll. There are six possible results from rolling a single die. So, each side has an equal chance of happening. So, the probability of any number coming up is 1 out of 6.

> **Review Video: <u>Simple Probability</u>**
> Visit ***mometrix.com/academy*** *and enter **Code: 212374***

<u>Terms often used in probability</u>:
Simple event – a situation that produces results of some sort (e.g., a coin toss)

Compound event – event that involves two or more items (e.g., rolling a pair of dice and taking the sum)

Outcome – a possible result in an experiment or event (e.g., heads and tails)

Desired outcome (or success) – an outcome that meets a particular set of requirements (e.g., a roll of 1 or 2 when we want a number that is less than 3)

Independent events – two or more events whose outcomes do not affect one another (e.g., two coins tossed at the same time)

Dependent events – two or more events whose outcomes affect one another (e.g., drawing two specific cards right after the other from the same deck)

Certain outcome – probability of outcome is 100% or 1

Impossible outcome – probability of outcome is 0% or 0

- 46 -

Mutually exclusive outcomes – two or more outcomes whose requirements cannot all be done in a single outcome. An example is a coin coming up heads and tails on the same toss.

Theoretical probability is the likelihood of a certain outcome happening for a given event. It can be known without actually doing the event.

Theoretical probability can be calculated as:

$$P(\text{probability of success}) = \frac{(\text{Desired Outcomes})}{(\text{Total Outcomes})}$$

Example:
There are 20 marbles in a bag and 5 are red. The theoretical probability of randomly selecting a red marble is 5 out of 20, (i.e., 5/20 = 1/4, 0.25, or 25%).

When we talk about probability, we mean theoretical probability most of the time. Experimental probability, or relative frequency, is the number of times an outcome happens in an experiment or a certain number of observed events.

Theoretical probability is based on what *should* happen. Experimental probability is based on what *has* happened. Experimental probability is calculated in the same way as theoretical. However, actual desired outcomes are used instead of possible desired outcomes.

Theoretical and experimental probability do not always line up with one another. Theoretical probability says that out of 20 coin tosses 10 should be heads. However, if we were actually to toss 20 coins, we might record just 5 heads. This doesn't mean that our theoretical probability is incorrect; it just means that this particular experiment had results that were different from what was predicted.

> **Review Video: Theoretical and Experimental Probability**
> *Visit **mometrix.com/academy** and enter **Code: 444349***

# Verbal

The Verbal test of the SSAT consists of a total of 60 questions (30 Synonyms and 30 Analogies).

## *Synonyms*

As part of your exam, you need to understand how words connect to each other. This is done with understanding words that mean the same thing or synonyms. For example, *dry* and *arid* are synonyms. There are pairs of words in English that can be called synonyms. Yet, they have somewhat different definitions.

For example, *wise* and *intelligent* can be used to describe someone who is very educated. So, you would be correct to call them synonyms. However, *wise* is used for good judgment. *Intelligent* is closer to good thinking.

Words should not be called synonyms when their differences are too great. For example, *hot* and *warm* are not synonyms because their meanings are too different. How do you know when two words are synonyms? First, try to replace one word for the other word. Then, be sure that the meaning of the sentence has not changed. Replacing *warm* for *hot* in a sentence gives a different meaning. *Warm* and *hot* may seem close in meaning. Yet, *warm* means that the temperature is normal. And, *hot* means that the temperature is very high.

> ➤ **Review Video: <u>Synonyms and Antonyms</u>**
> *Visit **mometrix.com/academy** and enter **Code: 105612***

**Synonyms**

For the Synonyms section, you will have one word and four choices for a synonym of that word. Before you look at the choices, try to think of a few words that could be a synonym for your question. Then, check the choices for a synonym of the question. Some words may seem close to the question, but you are looking for the best choice of a synonym. So, don't let your first reaction be your final decision.

<u>Example 1</u>
**Tranquil**:

A. Agitated
B. Nervous
C. Stable
D. Thrive
E. Violent

<u>Example 2</u>
**Agile**:

A. Cultivated
B. Dispirited
C. Frustrate
D. Rapid
E. Sluggish

<u>Example 3</u>
**Obstruction**:

A. Assistance
B. Barrier
C. Displace
D. Exhibition
E. Promotion


*Answers*
Example 1: C, Stable
Example 2: A, Rapid
Example 3: D, Barrier


# *Analogies*

## Determine the Relationship

As you try to decide on how the words in question are connected, don't jump to understand the meaning of the words. Instead, see if you can find the relationship between the two words. To understand the relationship, you can start by creating a sentence that links the two words and puts them into perspective. At first, try to use a simple sentence to find a connection.

Then, go through each answer choice and replace the words in the answer choices with the parts of your simple sentence. Depending on the question, you may need to make changes to your sentence to make it more specific.

<u>Example:</u>
Wood is to fire as

Simple Sentence: *Wood* feeds a *fire* as

Wood is to fire as
    A.   Farmer is to cow
    B.   Gasoline is to engine

Using the simple sentence, you would state "Farmer feeds a cow" which is correct. Yet, the next answer choice "Gasoline feeds an engine" is also true. So which is the correct answer? With this simple sentence, we need to be more specific.

*Specific Sentences*: "Wood feeds a fire and is consumed" / "Wood is burned in a fire"

These specific sentences show that answer choice (A) is incorrect and answer choice (B) is clearly correct. With the specific sentences, you have "Gasoline feeds an engine and is consumed" is correct. Also, "Farmer feeds a cow and is consumed" is clearly incorrect.

If your simple sentence seems correct with more than one answer choice, then keep making changes until only one answer choice makes sense.

> **Review Video:** <u>Determine the Relationship</u>
> *Visit mometrix.com/academy and enter Code:* **919115**

## Eliminating Similarities

This method works well in the Analogies section and the Synonyms section. You can start by looking over the answer choices and see what clues they provide. If there are any common relationships between the pairs of terms, then those answer choices have to be wrong.

Example:
Tough is to rugged as
    A. Soft is to hard
    B. Clear is to foggy
    C. Inhale is to exhale
    D. Throw is to catch
    E. Rigid is to taut

In this example, tough and rugged are synonyms. Also, the first four answer choices are antonyms. You may not realize that taut and rigid are synonyms. However, it has to be correct. The reason is that you know the other four answer choices all had the same relationship of being antonyms.

## Word Types

Example:
Gardener is to hedge as
    A. Wind is to rock
    B. Woodcarver is to stick

In this example, you could start with a simple sentence of "Gardener cuts away at hedges." Now, both answer choices seem correct with this sentence. For choice (A), you can say that "Wind cuts away at rocks" due to erosion. For choice (B), you can say that a "Woodcarver cuts away at sticks." The difference is that a gardener is a person, and a woodcarver is a person. However, the wind is a thing which makes answer choice (B) correct.

**Face Value**

When you are not sure about an answer, you should try to accept the problem at face value. Don't read too much into it. These problems will not ask you to make impossible comparisons. Truly, the SSAT test writers are not trying to throw you off with cheap tricks. If you have to make a stretch of the question to make a connection between the two terms, then you should start over and find another relationship. Don't make the problem more difficult. These are normal questions with differences in difficulty. Sometimes the terms that go together and their relationships may not be very clear. So, you will want to read over the question and answer choices carefully.

Example:

Odor is to smell as flavor is to

    A. believe
    B. know
    C. feel
    D. taste
    E. punish

Would a flavor be "punished," "known", "felt", "tasted", or "believed"? The analogy is about a synonym. So, answer choice D which is "taste" is a synonym of flavor and is the best answer.

**Read Carefully**

To understand the analogies, you need to read the terms and answer choices carefully. You can miss the question because you misread the terms. Each question here has only a few words, so you can spend time reading them carefully. Yet, you cannot forget your time limit of the section. So, don't spend too much time on one question. Just focus on reading carefully and be sure to read all of the choices. You may find an answer choice that seems correct. Yet, when you finish reading over the choices, you may find a better choice.

# Reading Comprehension

## Reading and Reasoning

**Types of Passages**

A **narrative** passage is a story that can be fiction or nonfiction (i.e., false or true). To be a narrative, the passage must have a few things. First, the text must have a plot (i.e., an order of events). Some narratives are written in a clear order, but this is not necessary. If the narrative is good, then you will find these events interesting. Second, a narrative has characters. These characters can be people, animals, or even lifeless items. As long as they play in the plot, they are a character. Third, a narrative passage often has figurative language. This is a tool that authors use to stir the imagination of readers with comparisons or comments. For example, a metaphor is a comparison between two things without using the words *like* or *as*. *He stood like a king* is not an example of a metaphor. *The moon was a frosty snowball* is an example of a metaphor. In reality, this is not true. Yet, the comparison gives a sense of calm to readers.

> ➤ **Review Video:** <u>Narratives</u>
> *Visit **mometrix.com/academy** and enter **Code: 280100***

An **expository** passage aims to inform or teach readers. The passage is nonfiction and usually centers around an easily explained topic. Often, an expository passage has helpful organizing words: *first, next, for example*, and *therefore*. These words let readers know where they are in the passage. While expository passages don't need to have difficult vocabulary and fancy writing, they are better with them. Yet, this can make it difficult to pay attention to an expository passage. Expository passages are not always about things that will interest you. Also, writers focus more on clearness and precision than with keeping the reader's interest. By careful reading, you will establish a good habit of focus when you read an expository passage.

> ➤ **Review Video:** <u>Expository Passages</u>
> *Visit **mometrix.com/academy** and enter **Code: 256515***

A **technical** passage is written to describe a complicated thing or action. Technical writing is common in medical and technology fields. In those fields, ideas of mathematics, science, and engineering need to be explained simply and clearly. A technical passage usually proceeds in a step-by-step order to help with understanding the passage. Technical passages often have clear headings and subheadings. These headings act like the organizing words in an expository passage: they let readers know where they are in a passage. Also, you will find that these passages divide sections up with numbers or letters.

Many technical passages look more like an outline than the paragraphs that you are reading right now. Depending on the audience, the amount of difficult vocabulary will change in a technical passage. Some technical passages try to stay away from language that readers will have to look up. However, some difficult vocabulary has to be used for writers to share their message.

> **Review Video: A Technical Passage**
> *Visit **mometrix.com/academy** and enter **Code: 478923***

A **persuasive** passage is written to change the mind of readers so that they agree with the author. The purpose of the passage may be very clear or very difficult to find. A persuasive passage wants to make an acceptable argument and win the trust of the reader. In some cases, a persuasive passage will be similar to an informative passage. Both passages make an argument and offer supporting details. However, a persuasive passage is more likely to appeal to the reader's feelings and make arguments based on opinions. Persuasive passages may not describe other points of view. So, when they do show other points of view, they may show favoritism to one side.

> **Review Video: Persuasive Text and Bias**
> *Visit **mometrix.com/academy** and enter **Code: 479856***

Persuasive passages will focus on one main argument and make many minor arguments (i.e., arguments that help the main argument) along the way. If you are going to accept the main argument, then you need to accept the minor arguments. So, the main argument will only be as strong as the minor arguments. These arguments should be rooted in fact and experience, not opinions. The best persuasive passages give enough supporting detail to back up arguments without confusing readers. Remember that a fact must be open to independent verification (i.e., the fact must be something that can be backed up by someone else). Also, statistics (i.e., data or figures are collected for study) are helpful only when they look at other choices. For example, a statistic on the number of bicycles sold would only be useful if it was taken over a limited time period and in a specific area. Good readers are careful with statistics because statistics can show what we want to see. Or, they can hide what we don't want to see. The writers of your test know that their passages will be met by questioning readers. So, your skill at questioning what you read will be a help in your exam.

> **Review Video: Persuasive Essay**
> *Visit **mometrix.com/academy** and enter **Code: 621428***

Opinions come from how we feel and what we think. Persuasive writers try often to appeal to the emotions (i.e., use or influence someone's feelings) of readers to make their arguments. You should always ask questions about this approach. You should ask questions because an author can pull you into accepting something that you don't want to accept. Sometimes these appeals can be used in a fair way. For example, some subjects cannot be totally addressed without an appeal to a reader's feelings. Think about an article on drunk driving. Some examples in the article will alarm or sadden readers because of the terrible outcome.

On the other hand, appeals to feelings are unacceptable when they try to mislead readers. For example, a presidential candidate (i.e., someone running for president) says that they care about the country. The candidate pushes you to make a connection. You care about the country as well and have positive feelings about the country. The candidate wants you to connect your positive feelings about the country with your thoughts about him or her. If you make more connections with the candidate, then you are likely to vote for him or her. Also, the person running for president hints that other candidates do not care about the country.

Another common and unacceptable appeal to feelings is the use of loaded language. Calling a religious person a *fanatic* or a person interested in the environment a *tree hugger* are examples of loaded language.

**Organization of the Passage**

The way a passage is organized can help readers to understand the author's purpose and his or her conclusions. There are many ways to organize a passage, and each one has an important use.

Some nonfiction texts are organized to **present a problem** followed by a solution. For this type of passage, the problem is explained before the solution is given. When the problem is well known, the solution may be given in a few sentences at the beginning. Other passages may focus on the solution, and the problem will be talked about a few times. Some passages will outline many solutions to a problem. This will leave you to choose among the possible solutions. If authors have loyalty to one solution, they may not describe some of the other solutions. Be careful with the author's plan when reading a problem-solution passage. When you know the author's point of view, you can make a better judgment of the author's solution.

Sometimes authors will organize information clearly for you to follow and locate the information. However, this is not always the case with passages in an exam. Two common ways to order a passage are cause and effect and chronological order. When using **chronological order** (i.e., a plan that moves in order from the first step to the last), the author gives information in the order that the event happened. For example, biographies are written in chronological order. The person's birth and childhood are first. Their adult life is next. The events leading up to the person's death are last.

In **cause and effect**, an author shows one thing that makes something else happen. For example, if one were to go to bed very late and wake up very early, then they would be tired in the morning. The cause is lack of sleep, with the effect of being tired the next day.

Finding the cause-and-effect relationships in a passage can be tricky. Often, these relationships come with certain words or terms. When authors use words like *because*, *since*, *in order*, and *so*, they are describing a cause and effect relationship. Think about the sentence: *He called her because he needed the homework*. This is a simple causal relationship. The cause was his need for the homework, and the effect was his phone call. Yet, not all cause and effect relationships are marked like this. Think about the sentences: *He called her. He needed the homework.* When the cause-and-effect relationship does not come with a keyword, the relationship can be known by asking why. For example, He called her: *why?* The answer is in the next sentence: He needed the homework.

When authors try to change the minds of readers, they may use cause-and-effect relationships. However, these relationships should not always be taken at face value. To read a persuasive essay well, you need to judge the cause-and-effect relationships. For

- 54 -

example, imagine an author wrote the following: *The parking deck has not been making money because people want to ride their bikes.* The relationship is clear: the cause is that people want to ride their bikes. The effect is that the parking deck has not been making money. However, you should look at this argument again. Maybe there are other reasons that the parking deck was not a success: a bad economy, too many costs, etc.

Many passages follow the **compare-and-contrast** model. In this model, the similarities and differences between two ideas or things are reviewed. A review of the similarities between ideas is called comparison. In a perfect comparison, the author shows ideas or things in the same way. If authors want to show the similarities between football and baseball, then they can list the equipment and rules for each game. Think about the similarities as they appear in the passage and take note of any differences.

Careful thinking about ideas and conclusions can seem like a difficult task. You can make this task easy by understanding the basic parts of ideas and writing skills. Looking at the way that ideas link to others is a good way for you to begin. Sometimes authors will write about two ideas that are against each other. Other times, an author will support a topic, and another author will argue against the topic. The review of these rival ideas is known as **contrast**. In contrast, all ideas should be presented clearly. If the author does favor a side, you need to read carefully to find where the author shows or hides this favoritism. Also, as you read the passage, you should write out how one side views the other.

**Purposes for Writing**

To be a careful reader, pay attention to the author's **position** and purpose. Even passages that seem fair and equal--like textbooks--have a position or bias (i.e., the author is unfair or inaccurate with opposing ideas). Readers need to take these positions into account when considering the author's message. Authors who appeal to feelings or like one side of an argument make their position clear. Authors' positions may be found in what they write and in what they don't write. Normally, you would want to review other passages on the same topic to understand the author's position. However, you are in the middle of an exam. So, look for language and arguments that show a position.

> ➤ **Review Video: Author's Position**
> *Visit **mometrix.com/academy** and enter **Code: 478923***

Sometimes, finding the **purpose** of an author is easier than finding his or her position. In most cases, the author has no interest in hiding his or her purpose. A passage for entertainment will be written to please readers. Most stories are written to entertain. However, they can inform or persuade. Informative texts are easy to recognize. The most difficult purpose of a text to determine is persuasion. In persuasion, the author wants to make the purpose hard to find. When you learn that the author wants to persuade, you should be skeptical of the argument. Persuasive passages try to establish an entertaining tone and hope to amuse you into agreement. On the other hand, an informative tone may be used to seem fair and equal to all sides.

An author's purpose is clear often in the organization of the text (e.g., section headings in bold font points for an informative passage). However, you may not have this organization in your passages. So, if authors make their main idea clear from the beginning, then their

*Copyright © Mometrix Media. You have been licensed one copy of this document for personal use only. Any other reproduction or redistribution is strictly prohibited. All rights reserved.*

likely purpose is to inform. If the author makes a main argument and gives minor arguments for support, then the purpose is probably to persuade. If the author tells a story, then his or her purpose is most likely to entertain. If the author wants your attention more than to persuade or inform, then his or her purpose is most likely to entertain. You must judge authors on how well they reach their purpose. In other words, think about the type of passage (e.g., technical, persuasive, etc.) that the author has written and if the author has followed the demands of the passage type.

> ➤ **Review Video: Purpose of an Author**
> *Visit* **mometrix.com/academy** *and enter* **Code: 497555**

The author's purpose will influence his or her writing approach and the reader's reaction. In a persuasive essay, the author wants to prove something to readers. There are several important marks of persuasive writing. Opinion given as fact is one mark. When authors try to persuade readers, they give their opinions as if they were facts. Readers must be on guard for statements that sound like facts but cannot be tested. Another mark of persuasive writing is the appeal to feelings. An author will try to play with the feelings of readers by appealing to their ideas of what is right and wrong. When an author uses strong language to excite the reader's feelings, then the author may want to persuade. Many times, a persuasive passage will give an unfair explanation of other sides. Or, the other sides are not shown.

An **informative passage** is written to teach readers. Informative passages are almost always nonfiction. The purpose of an informative passage is to share information in the clearest way. In an informative passage, you may have a thesis statement (i.e., an argument on the topic of a passage that is explained by proof). A thesis statement is a sentence that normally comes at end of the first paragraph. Authors of informative passages are likely to put more importance on being clear. Informative passages do not normally appeal to the feelings. They often contain facts and figures. Informative passages almost never include the opinion of the author. However, you should know that there can be a bias in the facts. Sometimes, a persuasive passage can be like an informative passage. This is true when authors give their ideas as if they were facts.

**Entertainment passages** describe real or imagined people, places, and events. Entertainment passages are often stories or poems. So, figurative language is a common part of these passages. Often, an entertainment passage appeals to the imagination and feelings. Authors may persuade or inform in an entertainment passage. Or, an entertainment passage may cause readers to think differently about a subject.

When authors want to **share feelings,** they may use strong language. Authors may share feelings about a moment of great pain or happiness. Other times, authors will try to persuade readers by sharing feelings. Some phrases like *I felt* and *I sense* hint that the author is sharing feelings. Authors may share a story of deep pain or great joy. You must not be influenced by these stories. You need to keep some distance to judge the author's argument.

Almost all writing is descriptive. In one way or another, authors try to describe events, ideas, or people. Some texts are concerned only with **description**. A descriptive passage focuses on a single subject and seeks to explain the subject clearly. Descriptive passages contain many adjectives and adverbs (i.e., words that give a complete picture for you to imagine). Normally, a descriptive passage is informative. Yet, the passage may be persuasive or entertaining.

## Writing Devices

Authors will use different writing devices to make their message clear for readers. One of those devices is comparison and contrast. When authors show how two things are alike, they are **comparing** them. When authors describe how two things are different, they are **contrasting** them. The compare and contrast passage is a common part of nonfiction. Comparisons are known by certain words or phrases: *both, same, like, too,* and *as well*. Yet, contrasts may have words or phrases like *but, however, on the other hand, instead,* and *yet*. Of course, comparisons and contrasts may be understood without using those words or phrases. A single sentence may compare and contrast. Think about the sentence *Brian and Sheila love ice cream, but Brian loves vanilla and Sheila loves strawberry*. In one sentence, the author has described both a similarity (e.g., love of ice cream) and a difference (e.g., favorite flavor).

> ➤ **Review Video: Compare and Contrast**
> *Visit **mometrix.com/academy** and enter **Code: 798319***

Another regular writing device is **cause and effect**. A cause is an act or event that makes something happen. An effect is what comes from the cause. A cause and effect relationship is not always easy to find. So, there are some words and phrases that show causes: *since, because,* and *due to*. Words and phrases that show effects include *consequently, therefore, this lead(s) to, as a result*. For example, *Because the sky was clear, Ron did not bring an umbrella*. The cause is the clear sky, and the effect is that Ron did not bring an umbrella. Readers may find that the cause and effect relationship is not clear. For example, *He was late and missed the meeting*. This does not have any words that show cause or effect. Yet, the sentence still has a cause (e.g., he was late) and an effect (e.g., he missed the meeting).

Remember the chance for a single cause to have many effects (e.g., *Single cause*: Because you left your homework on the table, your dog eats the homework. *Many effects*: (1) As a result, you fail your homework. (2) Your parents do not let you see your friends. (3) You miss out on the new movie. (4) You miss holding the hand of an important person.).

Also, the chance of a single effect to have many causes (e.g.. *Single effect*: Alan has a fever. *Many causes*: (1) An unexpected cold front came through the area, and (2) Alan forgot to take his multi-vitamin.)

Now, an effect can become the cause of another effect. This is known as a cause and effect chain. (e.g., As a result of her hatred for not doing work, Lynn got ready for her exam. This led to her passing her test with high marks. Hence, her resume was accepted, and her application was accepted.)

**Point of view** has an important influence on a passage. A passage's point of view is how the author or a character sees or thinks about things. A point of view influences the events of a passage, the meetings among characters, and the ending to the story. For example, two characters watch a child ride a bike. Character one watches outside. Character two watches from inside a house. Both see the same event, yet they are around different noises, sights, and smells. Character one may see different things that happen outside that character two cannot see from inside. Also, point of view can be influenced by past events and beliefs. For example, if character one loves bikes, then she will remember how proud she is of the child. If character two is afraid of riding bikes, then he may not remember the event or fear for the child's safety.

In fiction, the two main points of view are first person and third person. The narrator is the person who tells a story's events. The protagonist is the main character of a story. If the narrator is the protagonist in a story, then the story is written in first-person. In first person, the author writes from the view of *I*. Third-person point of view is the most common among stories. With third person, authors refer to each character by using *he* or *she* and the narrator is not involved in the story. In third-person omniscient, the narrator is not a character in the story and tells the story of all of the characters at the same time.

> ➢ **Review Video: <u>Point of View</u>**
> *Visit **mometrix.com/academy** and enter **Code: 383336***

**Transitional words** and phrases are devices that guide readers through a passage. You may know the common transitions. Though you may not have thought about how they are used. Some transitional phrases (*after, before, during, in the middle of*) give information about time. Some hint that an example is about to be given (*for example, in fact, for instance*). Writers use transitions to compare (*also, likewise*) and contrast (*however, but, yet*). Transitional words and phrases can point to addition (*and, also, furthermore, moreover*) and understood relationships (*if, then, therefore, as a result, since*). Finally, transitional words and phrases can separate the chronological steps (*first, second, last*).

> ➢ **Review Video: <u>Transitional Words and Phrases</u>**
> *Visit **mometrix.com/academy** and enter **Code: 197796***

**Understanding a Passage**

One of the most important skills in reading comprehension is finding **topics** and **main ideas.** There is a small difference between these two. The topic is the subject of a passage (i.e., what the passage is all about). The main idea is the most important argument being made by the author. The topic is shared in a few words while the main idea needs a full sentence to be understood. As an example, a short passage might have the topic of penguins, and the main idea could be written as *Penguins are different from other birds in many ways.*

In most nonfiction writing, the topic and the main idea will be stated clearly. Sometimes, they will come in a sentence at the very beginning or end of the passage. When you want to know the topic, you may find it in the first sentence of each paragraph. A body paragraph's first sentence is often--but not always--the main topic sentence. The topic sentence gives you a summary of the ideas in the paragraph. You may find that the topic or main idea is not given clearly. So, you must read every sentence of the passage. Then, try to come up with an overall idea from each sentence.

Note: A thesis statement is not the same as the main idea. The main idea gives a brief, general summary of a text. The thesis statement gives a clear idea on an issue that is backed up with evidence.

> ➤ **Review Video:** <u>Topics and Main Ideas</u>
> *Visit **mometrix.com/academy** and enter **Code: 691033***

The main idea is the umbrella argument of a passage. So, **supporting details** back up the main idea. To show that a main idea is correct, authors add details that prove their idea. All passages contain details. However, they are supporting details when the details help an argument in the passage. Supporting details are found in informative and persuasive texts. Sometimes they will come with terms like *for example* or *for instance.* Or, they will be numbered with terms like *first*, *second*, and *last.* You should think about how the author's supporting details back up his or her main idea. Supporting details can be correct, yet they may help the author's main idea. Sometimes supporting details can seem helpful. However, they may be useless when they are based on opinions.

> ➤ **Review Video:** <u>Supporting Details</u>
> *Visit **mometrix.com/academy** and enter **Code: 396297***

An example of a main idea: *Giraffes live in the Serengeti of Africa.* A supporting detail about giraffes could be: *A giraffe in the Serengeti benefits from a long neck by reaching twigs and leaves on tall trees.* The main idea gives the general idea that the text is about giraffes. The supporting detail gives a clear fact about how the giraffes eat.

A **theme** is an issue, an idea, or a question raised by a passage. For example, a theme of *Cinderella* is determination as Cinderella serves her step-sisters and step-mother. Passages may have many themes, and you must be sure to find only themes that you are asked to find. One common mark of themes is that they give more questions than answers. Authors try to push readers to consider themes in other ways. You can find themes by asking about the general problems that the passage is addressing. A good way to find a theme is to begin reading with a question in mind (e.g., How does this passage use the theme of love?) and to look for answers to that question.

> ➤ **Review Video:** <u>Theme</u>
> *Visit **mometrix.com/academy** and enter **Code: 732074***

**Evaluating a Passage**

When you read informational passages, you need to make a conclusion from the author's writing. You can **identify a logical conclusion** (i.e., find a conclusion that makes sense) to know whether you agree or disagree with an author. Coming to this conclusion is like making an inference. You combine the information from the passage with what you already know. From the passage's information and your knowledge, you can come to a conclusion that makes sense. One way to have a conclusion that makes sense is to take notes of all the author's points. When the notes are organized, they may point to the logical conclusion.

Another way to reach conclusions is to ask if the author's passage raises any helpful questions. Sometimes you will be able to draw many conclusions from a passage. Yet, these may be conclusions that were never imagined by the author. Therefore, find reasons in the passage for the conclusions that you make.

> ➢ **Review Video: Identifying a Logical Conclusion**
> *Visit **mometrix.com/academy** and enter **Code: 281653***

**Text evidence** is the information that supports a main argument or minor argument. This evidence, or proof, can lead you to a conclusion. Information used as text evidence is clear, descriptive, and full of facts. Supporting details give evidence to back-up an argument.

For example, a passage may state that winter occurs during opposite months in the Northern hemisphere (i.e., north of the equator) and Southern hemisphere (i.e., south of the equator). Text evidence for this claim may include a list of countries where winter occurs in opposite months. Also, you may be given reasons that winter occurs at different times of the year in these hemispheres (e.g., the tilt of the Earth as it rotates around the sun).

> ➢ **Review Video: Text Evidence**
> *Visit **mometrix.com/academy** and enter **Code: 486236***

A reader should always draw conclusions from passages. Sometimes conclusions are implied (i.e., information that is assumed) from written information. Other times the information is **stated directly** within the passage. You should try to draw conclusions from information stated in a passage. Furthermore, you should always read through the entire passage before drawing conclusions. Many readers expect the author's conclusions at the beginning or the end of the passage. However, many texts do not follow this format.

**Implications** are things that the author does not say directly. Yet, you can assume from what the author does say. For example, *I stepped outside and opened my umbrella. By the time I got to work, the cuffs of my pants were soaked.* The author never says that it is raining. However, you can conclude that this is information is implied. Conclusions from implications must be well supported by the passage. To draw a conclusion, you should have many pieces of proof. Yet, let's say that you have only one piece. Then, you need to be sure that there is no other possible explanation than your conclusion. Practice drawing conclusions from implications in real life events to improve your skills.

**Outlining** the information in a passage should be a well-known skill to readers. A good outline will show the pattern of the passage and lead to better conclusions. A common outline calls for the main ideas of the passage to be listed in the order that they come. Then, beneath each main idea, you can list the minor ideas and details. An outline does not need to include every detail from the passage. However, the outline should show everything that is important to the argument.

Another helpful tool is the skill of **summarizing** information. This process is similar to creating an outline. First, a summary should define the main idea of the passage. The summary should have the most important supporting details or arguments. Summaries can be unclear or wrong because they do not stay true to the information in the passage. A helpful summary should have the same message as the passage.

Ideas from a passage can be organized using **graphic organizers**. A graphic organizer reduces information to a few key points. A graphic organizer like a timeline may have an event listed for each date on the timeline. However, an outline may have an event listed under a key point that happens in the passage.

You need to make a graphic organizer that works best for you. Whatever helps you remember information from a passage is what you need to use. A spider-map is another example. This map takes a main idea from the story and places it in a bubble. From one main idea bubble, you put supporting points that connect to the main idea. A Venn diagram groups information as separate or connected with some overlap.

➤ **Review Video: Graphic Organizers**
*Visit **mometrix.com/academy** and enter **Code: 665513***

**Paraphrasing** is another method that you can use to understand a passage. To paraphrase, you put what you have read into your own words. Or, you can *translate* what the author shared into your words by including as many details as you can.

**Responding to a Passage**

One part of being a good reader is making predictions. A **prediction** is a guess about what will happen next. Readers make predictions from what they have read and what they already know. For example: *Staring at the computer screen in shock, Kim reached for the glass of water.* The sentence leaves you to think that she is not looking at the glass. So, you may guess that Kim is going to knock over the glass. Yet, in the next sentence, you may read that Kim does not knock over the glass. As you have more information, be ready for your predictions to change.

➤ **Review Video: Predictions**
*Visit **mometrix.com/academy** and enter **Code: 437248***

*Test-taking tip*: To respond to questions that ask about predictions, your answer should come from the passage.

You will be asked to understand text that gives ideas without stating them directly. An **inference** is something that is implied but not stated directly by the author. For example: *After the final out of the inning, the fans were filled with joy and rushed the field.* From this sentence, you can infer that the fans were watching baseball and their team won. You should not use information outside of the passage before making inferences. As you practice making inferences, you will find that they need all of your attention.

➤ **Review Video: Inference**
*Visit **mometrix.com/academy** and enter **Code: 379203***

*Test-taking tip*: When asked about inferences, look for context clues. Context is what surrounds the words and sentences that add explanation or information to an unknown piece. An answer can be *true* but not *correct*. The context clues will help you find the answer that is best. When asked for the implied meaning of a statement, you should locate the statement first. Then, read the context around the statement. Finally, look for an answer with a similar phrase.

For your exam, you must be able to find a text's **sequence** (i.e., the order that things happen). When the sequence is very important to the author, the passage comes with signal words: *first*, *then*, *next*, and *last*. However, a sequence can be implied. For example, *He walked through the garden and gave water and fertilizer to the plants.* Clearly, the man did not walk through the garden at the beginning. First, he found water. Then, he collected fertilizer. Next, he walked through the garden. Finally, he gave water and fertilizer to the plants. Passages do not always come in a clear sequence. Sometimes they begin at the end. Or, they can start over at the beginning. You can strengthen your understanding of the passage by taking notes to understand the sequence.

## Building a Vocabulary

There is more to a word than the dictionary definition. The **denotative** meaning of a word is the actual meaning found in a dictionary. For example, a house and a home are places where people live. The **connotative meaning** is what comes to mind when you think of a word. For example, a house may be a simple, solid building. Yet, a home may be a comfortable, welcoming place where a family stays. Most non-fiction is fact-based with no use of figurative language. So, you can assume that the writer will use denotative meanings. In fiction, drama, and poetry, the author may use the connotative meaning. Use context clues to know if the author is using the denotative or connotative meaning of a word.

> **Review Video:** <u>Denotative and Connotative Meanings</u>
> *Visit* ***mometrix.com/academy*** *and enter* ***Code: 736707***

Readers of all levels will find new words in passages. The best way to define a word in **context** is to think about the words that are around the unknown word. For example, nouns that you don't know may be followed by examples that give a definition. Think about this example: *Dave arrived at the party in hilarious garb: a leopard-print shirt, buckskin pants, and tennis shoes.* If you didn't know the meaning of garb, you could read the examples (i.e., a leopard-print shirt, buckskin pants, and tennis shoes) and know that *garb* means *clothing*. Examples will not always be this clear. Try another example: *Parsley, lemon, and flowers were just a few of items he used as garnishes.* The word *garnishes* is explained by parsley, lemon, and flowers. From this one sentence, you may know that the items are used for decoration. Are they decorating a food plate or an ice table with meat? You would need the other sentences in the paragraph to know for sure.

> **Review Video:** <u>Context</u>
> *Visit* ***mometrix.com/academy*** *and enter* ***Code: 613660***

Also, you can use contrasts to define an unfamiliar word in context. In many sentences, authors will not describe the unfamiliar word directly. Instead, they will describe the opposite of the unfamiliar word. So, you are given some information that will bring you closer to defining the word. For example: *Despite his intelligence, Hector's bad posture made him look obtuse. Despite* means that Hector's posture is at odds with his intelligence. The author explains that Hector's posture does not prove his intelligence. So, *obtuse* must mean *unintelligent.* Another example: *Even with the horrible weather, we were beatific about our trip to Alaska.* The weather is described as *horrible.* So, *beatific* must mean something positive.

Sometimes, there will be very few context clues to help you define an unknown word. When this happens, **substitution** is a helpful tool. First, try to think of some synonyms for the words. Then, use those synonyms in place of the unknown words. If the passage makes sense, then the substitution has given some information about the unknown word. For example: *Frank's admonition rang in her ears as she climbed the mountain.* Don't know the definition of *admonition*? Then, try some substitutions: *vow, promise, advice, complaint,* or *compliment.* These words hint that an *admonition* is some sort of message. Once in a while substitution can get you a precise definition.

Usually, you can define an unfamiliar word by looking at the descriptive words in the context. For example: *Fred dragged the recalcitrant boy kicking and screaming up the stairs.* The words *dragged, kicking,* and *screaming* all hint that the boy hates going up the stairs. So, you may think that *recalcitrant* means something like unwilling or protesting. In this example, an unfamiliar adjective was identified.

**Description** is used more to define an unfamiliar noun than unfamiliar adjectives. For example: *Don's wrinkled frown and constantly shaking fist labeled him as a curmudgeon.* Don is described as having a *wrinkled frown* and *constantly shaking fist.* This hints that a *curmudgeon* must be a grumpy, old man. Contrasts do not always give detailed information about the unknown word. However, they do give you some clues to understand the word.

Many words have more than one definition. So, you may not know how the word is being used in a sentence. For example, the verb *cleave* can mean *join* or *separate.* When you see this word, you need to pick the definition that makes the most sense. For example: *The birds cleaved together as they flew from the oak tree.* The use of the word *together* hints that *cleave* is being used to mean *join.* Another example: *Hermione's knife cleaved the bread cleanly.* A knife cannot join bread together. So, the word must hint at separation. Learning the purpose of a word with many meanings needs the same tricks as defining an unknown word. Look for context clues and think about the substituted words.

## Critical Thinking Skills

**Opinions and Facts**

Critical thinking skills are mastered by understanding the types of writing and the purposes of authors. Every author writes for a purpose. To know the purpose of authors and how they accomplish their purpose has two important steps. First, think carefully about their writing. Then, determine if you agree with their conclusions.

Readers must always be aware of the difference between fact and opinion. A **fact** can be proved or disproved. An **opinion** is the author's personal thoughts or feelings. So, an opinion cannot be proved or disproved.

For example, an author writes that the distance from New York City to Boston is about two hundred miles. The author is giving a fact. We can drive to Boston from New York City and

*Copyright © Mometrix Media. You have been licensed one copy of this document for personal use only. Any other reproduction or redistribution is strictly prohibited. All rights reserved.*

find that it took about 200 miles. However, another author writes that New York City is too crowded. This author is giving an opinion. The reason that this is an opinion is that there is no independent measurement for overpopulation. You may think that where you live is overcrowded. Yet, someone else may say that more people can live in your area.

An opinion may come with words like *believe*, *think*, or *feel*. Know that an opinion can be backed up with facts. For example, someone may give the population density (i.e., the number of people living for each square mile) of New York City as a reason for an overcrowded population. An opinion backed up with facts can seem convincing. However, this does not mean that you should accept the argument.

Use these steps to know the difference between fact and opinion. First, think about the type of source that is presenting information (e.g., Is this information coming from someone or something that is trusted by me and others?). Next, think about the information that backs up a claim (e.g., Are the details for the argument opinions or facts?). Then, think about the author's motivation to have a certain point of view on a topic (e.g., Why does this person care about this issue?).

For example, a group of scientists tests the value of a product. The results are likely to be full of facts. Now, compare the group of scientists to a company. The company sells a product and says that their products are good. The company says this because they want to sell their product. Yet, the scientists use the scientific method (i.e. an independent way of proving ideas and questions) to prove the value of the product. The company's statements about the product may be true. But, the group of scientists *proves* the value of the product.

> **Review Video: Fact or Opinion**
> *Visit **mometrix.com/academy** and enter **Code: 870899***

When writers try to persuade, they make mistakes often in their thinking patterns and writing choices. These patterns and choices are important for making an informed decision. Authors show their bias when they ignore fair counterarguments or twist opposing points of view. A **bias** is obvious when the author is unfair or inaccurate with opposing ideas. Remember that a bias may be correct. However, authors will not be correct because of their bias. A **stereotype** is like a bias. Yet, a stereotype is used only with a group or place. Stereotyping is thought to be wrong because the practice pairs uninformed ideas with people or places. Be very careful with authors who stereotype. These uninformed ideas almost always show the author's ignorance and lack of curiosity.

> **Review Video: Bias and Stereotype**
> *Visit **mometrix.com/academy** and enter **Code: 456336***

# Literature

## Literary Genres

**Fiction** is a general term for any type of narrative that is invented or imagined. Your exam will have a passage that was written for your test. Or, a passage may be taken from a published work. During your exam, you may recognize a passage that you have read. In this case, you still need to follow the rule of reading the passage once. Then, go to the test questions. This rule applies to the other genres as well. Now, let's start with fiction.

Fiction has many subgroups, but the genre can be put into three main subgroups:
- **Short stories**: a fictional passage that has fewer than 20,000 words. Short stories have only a few characters and normally have one important event. The short story began in magazines in the late 1800s.
- **Novels**: longer works of fiction that may have many characters and a far-reaching plot. The attention may be on an event, action, social problem, or an experience. Note: novels may be written like poetry.
- **Novellas**: a work of fiction that is longer than a short story. But, the work is not longer than a novel. Novellas may also be called short novels or novelettes. They come from the German tradition and have increased in popularity across the world.

Many elements influence a work of fiction. Some important ones are:
- Speech and dialogue: Dialogue is the communication among characters. These characters may speak for themselves. Or, the narrator may share what a character has spoken. This speech or dialogue may seem possible. Or, you may find that the speech is imaginary. The choice depends on the author's purpose.
- Thoughts and Internal Conflict: External conflict is the action and events that are around the character. Internal conflict is the thoughts and feelings that bother a character. This conflict that happens inside a character is used to develop the plot. Or, the internal conflict can be used to show the growth or lack of growth in a character.
- Dramatic involvement: Some narrators want readers to join with the events of the story (e.g., Thornton Wilder's *Our Town*). Other authors try to separate themselves from readers with figurative language.
- Action: The events that continue the plot. Also, this can show new meetings among characters.
- Duration: The amount of time that passes in the passage may be long or short. If the author gives an amount of time (e.g., three days later), then that information is important to remember.
- Setting and description: Is the setting (i.e., time and place within the passage) important to the plot or characters? How are the action scenes described?
- Themes: This is any point of view or topic that is given constant attention.
- Symbolism: Authors may share what they mean through imagery and other figurative devices. For example, smoke can be a symbol of danger, and doves are symbols of peace.

> ➤ **Review Video:** <u>Elements that Influence Fiction</u>
> *Visit **mometrix.com/academy** and enter Code:* **789211**

**Plot lines** are one way to show the information given in a story. Every plot line has the same stages. You can find each of these stages in every story that you read. These stages include the introduction, rising action, conflict, climax, falling action, and resolution. The introduction tells you the point of the story and sets up the plot. The rising action is the events that lead up to the conflict (i.e., an internal or external problem) with the climax at the peak. The falling action is the events that come after the climax of the conflict. The resolution is the conclusion and may have the final solution to the problem in the conflict. A plot line looks like this:

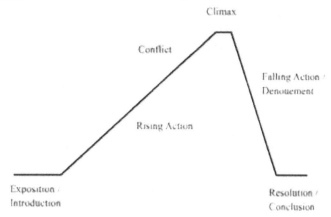

> ➤ **Review Video: Plot Lines**
> *Visit* ***mometrix.com/academy*** *and enter* ***Code:*** **944011**

Most passages put events in chronological order. However, some authors may use an unusual order to have a particular influence on readers. For example, many of the Greek epics begin *in medias res* (i.e., in the middle of things). The passage begins with an introduction to the climax. Then, the author goes to the beginning and shares how events came to that climax. This order is found in many mystery novels. First, a crime is committed. Then, a detective must go back and piece together the events that led to the crime. As you read, try to keep in mind the cause-and-effect relationships that shape the story. A cause must come before an effect. So, use an outline of the different causes and effects in a passage. Be sure that this outline will show the correct chronological order. Remember that the order of events in a story is not always the order that they happened.

The **narrator** can give insight about the purpose of the work and the main themes and ideas. There are important questions to ask about understanding the voice and role of the narrator:

- Who is the narrator of the passage? What is the narrator's perspective: first person or third person? Is the narrator involved in the plot? Are there changes in narrators?
- Does the narrator explain things in the passage? Or, are things explained with the plot and events? Does the narrator give special description to one character or event and not to others? A narrator may express approval or disapproval about a character or events in the work.
- Tone is the attitude of a character through his or her words. If the narrator is involved in the story, how is the narrator addressing others? Is the tone casual or formal? Close or distant? Does the narrator's vocabulary give any information about the narrator?

> ➤ **Review Video: <u>The Narrator</u>**
> *Visit **mometrix.com/academy** and enter **Code: 742528***

A **character** is someone or something that is connected closely with the plot and growth of the passage. As characters grow in a story, they move along the plot line. Characters can be named as flat, round, or stock. Flat characters are simple individuals that are known for one or two things. Often, they are supporting characters to round characters. Minor flat characters are stock characters that fill out the story without influencing the outcome. Round characters--usually protagonists--are crucial to the story. They are explored widely and explained in much detail. If characters change or develop, they can be known as static or dynamic. Static characters either do not change or change very little in a passage. In other words, who they are at the beginning is who they are at the end. However, dynamic characters change over the course of a passage. In other words, who they are at the beginning is not at all who they are at the end.

> ➤ **Review Video: <u>Characters</u>**
> *Visit **mometrix.com/academy** and enter **Code: 429493***

Prose is ordinary spoken language as opposed to verse (i.e., language with metric patterns). The everyday, normal communication is known as prose and can be found in textbooks, memos, reports, articles, short stories, and novels. Distinguishing characteristics of prose include:

- Some sort of rhythm may be present, but there is no formal arrangement.
- The common unit of organization is the sentence which may include literary devices of repetition and balance.
- There must be coherent relationships among sentences.

**Poetry**, or verse, is the manipulation of language with respect to meaning, meter, sound, and rhythm. Lines of poetry vary in length and scope, and they may or may not rhyme. Related groups of lines are called stanzas and may be any length. Some poems are as short as a few lines, and some are as long as a book.

A line of poetry can be any length and can have any metrical pattern. A line is determined by the physical position of the words on a page. A line is one group of words that follows the next group in a stanza. Lines may or may not have punctuation at the end depending on the need for punctuation. Consider the following example from John Milton:

"When I consider how my light is spent,
E're half my days, in this dark world and wide,"

A stanza is a group of lines. The grouping denotes a relationship among the lines. A stanza can be any length, but the separation of lines into different stanzas indicates an intentional pattern created by the poet. The breaks between stanzas indicate a change of subject or thought. As a group of lines, the stanza is a melodic unit that can be analyzed for metrical patterns and rhyme patterns. Stanzas of a certain length have been named to indicate an author's purpose with a form of poetry. A few examples include the couplet (two lines), the tercet (three lines), and the quatrain (four lines).

Another important genre is **drama**: a play written to be spoken aloud. The drama is in many ways inseparable from performance. Ideally, reading drama involves using imagination to visualize and re-create the play with characters and settings. Readers stage the play in their imagination and watch characters interact and developments unfold. Sometimes this involves simulating a theatrical presentation, while other times you need to imagine the events. In either case, you are imagining the unwritten to recreate the dramatic experience. Novels present some of the same problems, but a narrator will provide much more information about the setting, characters, inner dialogues, and many other supporting details. In drama, much of this is missing, and you are required to use your powers of projection and imagination to understand the dramatic work. There are many empty spaces in dramatic texts that must be filled by the reader to appreciate the work.

> **Review Video:** Dramas
*Visit **mometrix.com/academy** and enter **Code: 216060***

# Figurative Language

When authors want to share their message in a creative way, they use figurative language devices. Learning these devices will help you understand what you read. **Figurative language** is communication that goes beyond the actual meaning of a word or phrase. **Descriptive language** that awakens imagery in the reader's mind is one type of figurative language. Exaggeration is another type of figurative language. Also, when you compare two things, you are using figurative language. Similes and metaphors are the two main ways of comparing things. An example of a simile: *The child howled like a coyote when her mother told her to pick up the toys*. In this example, the child's howling is compared to a coyote. This helps the reader understand the sound being made by the child.

A **figure of speech** is a word or phrase that is not a part of straightforward, everyday language. Figures of speech are used for emphasis, fresh expression, or clearness. However, clearness of a passage may be incomplete with the use of these devices. For example: *I am going to crown you.*
The author may mean:
- I am going to place a real crown on your head.
- I am going to make you king or queen of this area.
- I am going to punch you in the head with my fist.
- I am going to put a second checker's piece on top of your checker piece to show that it has become a king.

> ➤ **Review Video: Figure of Speech**
> *Visit mometrix.com/academy and enter Code:* **111295**

An **allusion** is a comparison of someone or something to a person or event in history or literature. Allusions that point to people or events that are a part of today's culture are called topical allusions. Those that name a specific person are known as personal allusions. For example, *His desire for power was his Achilles' heel*. This example points to Achilles: a notable hero in Greek mythology who was thought to be invincible (i.e., cannot be hurt) except for his heels. Today, the term *Achilles' heel* points to an individual's weakness.

> ➤ **Review Video: Allusion**
> *Visit mometrix.com/academy and enter Code:* **294065**

A **metaphor** is the comparison of one thing with a different thing. For example: *The bird was an arrow flying across the sky*. In this sentence, the arrow is compared to a bird. The metaphor asks you to think about the bird in another way. Let's continue with this metaphor for a bird. You are asked to view the bird's flight as the flight of an arrow. So, you may imagine the flight to be quick and purposeful.

Metaphors allow the author to describe a thing without being direct. Remember that the thing being described will not always be mentioned directly by the author. Think about a forest in winter: *Swaying skeletons reached for the sky and groaned as the wind blew through them.* In this sentence, the author uses *skeletons* as a metaphor for trees without leaves.

> ➤ **Review Video: Metaphor**
> *Visit mometrix.com/academy and enter Code:* **133295**

**Hyperbole** is overstatement or exaggeration. For example: *He jumped ten feet in the air when he heard the good news*. Obviously, no person can jump ten feet in the air without help. The author exaggerates because the hyperbole shares a lot of feeling. Let's say that the author shared: *He jumped when he heard the good news*. With this information, you might think that the character is not feeling very excited. Hyperbole can be dangerous if the author does not exaggerate enough. For example: *He jumped two feet in the air when he heard the good news*. You may think that the author is writing a fact. Be careful with confusing hyperboles. Some test questions may have a hyperbole and a fact listed in the answer choices.

**Understatement** is the opposite of hyperbole. The device discounts or downplays something. Think about someone who climbs Mount Everest. Then, they say that the journey was *a little stroll*. As with other types of figurative language, understatement has a range of uses. The device may show self-defeat or modesty as in the Mount Everest example. However, some may think of understatement as false modesty (i.e., an attempt to bring attention to you or a situation). For example, a woman is praised on her diamond engagement ring. The woman says, *Oh, this little thing?* Her understatement might be heard as stuck-up or unfeeling.

> ➤ **Review Video: <u>Hyperbole and Understatement</u>**
> *Visit **mometrix.com/academy** and enter **Code: 308470***

A **simile** is a comparison that needs the separation words *like* or *as*. Some examples: *The sun was like an orange*, *eager as a beaver*, and *quick as a mountain goat*. Because a simile includes *like* or a*s*, the comparison uses a different tone than a simple description of something. For example: *the house was like a shoebox*. The tone is different than the author saying that the house *was* a shoebox.

> ➤ **Review Video: <u>Simile</u>**
> *Visit **mometrix.com/academy** and enter **Code: 642949***

**Personification** is the explanation of a nonhuman thing with human attributes. The basic purpose of personification is to describe something in a way that readers will understand. An author says that a tree *groans* in the wind. The author does not mean that the tree is giving a low, pained sound from a mouth. However, the author means that the tree is making a noise like a human groan. Of course, this personification creates a tone of sadness or suffering. A different tone would be made if the author said that the tree *sways* or *dances*.

> ➤ **Review Video: <u>Personification</u>**
> *Visit **mometrix.com/academy** and enter **Code: 260066***

**Irony** is a statement that hints at the opposite of what you expect. In other words, the device is used when an author or character says one thing but means another. For example, imagine a man who is covered in mud and dressed in tattered clothes. He walks in his front door to meet his wife. Then, his wife asks him, "How was your day?" He says, "Great!" The man's response to his wife is an example of irony. There is a difference between irony and sarcasm. Sarcasm is similar to irony. However, sarcasm is hurtful for the person receiving the sarcastic statement. A sarcastic statement points to the foolishness of a person to believe that a false statement is true.

> ➤ **Review Video: <u>Irony</u>**
> *Visit **mometrix.com/academy** and enter **Code: 374204***

As you read, you will see more words in the context of a sentence. This will strengthen your vocabulary. Be sure to read on a regular basis. This practice will increase the number of ways that you have seen a word in context. Based on experience, a person can remember how a word was used in the past and use that knowledge for a new context. For example, a person may have seen the word *gull* used to mean a bird that is found near the seashore. However, a *gull* can be a person who is tricked easily. If the word in context is used for a person, you will see the insult. After all, gulls are not thought to be very smart. Use your knowledge of a word to find comparisons. This knowledge can be used to learn a new use of a word.

# Essay

**Practice Makes Prepared Writers**

Writing is a skill that continues to need development throughout a person's life. For some people, writing seems to be a natural gift. They rarely struggle with writer's block. When you read their papers, they have persuasive or entertaining ideas. For others, writing is an intimidating task that they endure. As you practice, you can improve your skills and be better prepared for writing a time-sensitive essay.

Remember that you are practicing for more than an exam. Two of the most valuable things in life are the abilities to read critically and to write clearly. When you work on evaluating the arguments of a passage and explain your thoughts well, you are developing skills that you will use for a lifetime. In this overview of essay writing, you will find strategies and tools that will prepare you to write better essays.

**Creative Writing**

Take time to read a story or hear stories read aloud and use those opportunities to learn more about how stories are put together. This offers a frame for you to talk about a story with others and will help you to write better stories. With each new story that you read, try to predict what could happen in the story. Try to understand the setting by picturing the scenes and sounds that are described and the behaviors of characters. Then, try to summarize the events to understand more of the story.

If you need more help with understanding a story, you can try to relate narrative characters and events to your own life. For example, when reading a story, you can ask the following: Who is the main character in the story? What happened first? What happened next? What happened at the end of the story? Where does this story take place? And what is the theme or point of this story?

Establish a Context
When writing a narrative, an author must establish the context of the story. In other words, the stage needs to be set for the story to begin. Sometimes this is done by establishing the setting of the story and then introducing a narrator and characters. A character or the narrator can be introduced first. A narrator and/or characters can be introduced in many ways: through the use of dialogue, through description, or through the reactions of the narrator or characters to an event. Whatever means an that you choose, the beginning of a narrative must be compelling for your audience.

*Discuss the introduction of the character in the following passage.*

> Her parents named her Milagro, which means "miracle" in Spanish, but they called her Milly. She was a premature baby, very tiny, and it was a miracle that she survived. That was the beginning of her good fortune.

The author uses a dramatic way to introduce the character. Readers are told that *Milagro* means "miracle" in Spanish. Readers are told that it was a miracle that Milagro survived her birth because she was born prematurely. The way Milagro is introduced is dramatic because the author uses information to hint at what may come next. This is a form of foreshadowing. The author has established an interesting beginning with how the character is introduced, and this captures the attention of readers.

*Point of View*
Point of view is the perspective from which writing occurs. There are several possibilities:

- *First person* is written so that the *I* of the story is a participant or observer. First-person narratives let narrators express inner feelings and thoughts. The narrator may be a close friend of the protagonist, or the narrator can be less involved with the main characters and plot.
- *Second person* is a device to draw the reader in more closely. It is really a variation or refinement of the first-person narrative. In some cases, a narrative combines both second-person and first-person voices, speaking of "you" and "I." When the narrator is also a character in the story, the narrative is better defined as first-person even though it also has addresses of "you."
- *Third person* may be either objective or subjective, and either omniscient or limited. Objective third-person narration does not include what the characters are thinking or feeling, while subjective third-person narration does include this information. The third-person omniscient narrator knows everything about all characters, including their thoughts and emotions; and all related places, times, and events. The third-person limited narrator may know everything about a particular character of focus, but is limited to that character. In other words, the narrator cannot speak about anything that character does not know.

Sequence of Events
The sequence of events in a narrative should follow naturally out of the action and the plot. Rather than being forced, the sequence should follow the natural flow of a dialogue or plot and enhance what happens in the story. The only time that the sequence is not in the order that events naturally happen is when an author decides to use the literary device called flashback. In this case the action does not flow in sequence; instead, the action jumps back and forth in time. Events in a narrative are extremely important in helping the reader understand the intent or message of a narrative, which is why it is important to take note of the way in which the plot unfolds.

Remember from the Reading section that a plot shows the order of a story. The introduction is the beginning of the story. Next, the rising action, conflict, climax, and falling action are the middle. Then, the resolution or conclusion is the ending. So, stay focused on the goal of writing a story that needs those main parts: a beginning, a middle, and an ending.

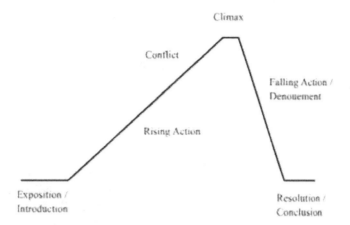

## Author Techniques

You can employ many techniques to make your narrative essay come alive in a fresh and interesting way. Dialogue is an important one. Often, dialogue is the means that helps readers understand what is happening and what a character is like. Equally important are the descriptions that you can use to help readers visualize a setting and what a character looks or acts like. Remember that you have limited time to write a whole story. So, don't be concerned with providing description for everything that you put in your story.

## Development of Characters

Characters are important to a story, and the problems that they face make a story interesting and complex. As you write your story, be sure to show more information about the characters through their actions. The actions of characters are important to advancing the plot because they show the different stages of the story. If your story teaches a lesson, hey also help the reader understand the theme or lesson that the story teaches.

## Conflict

A conflict is a problem that needs to be solved. Many stories include at least one conflict, and the characters' efforts to solve conflicts move the story forward. The protagonist is the character who has the main goal of solving the conflict. Conflicts can be external or internal to any of the characters. A major type of internal conflict is some inner personal battle that is called *man against himself*. This type of conflict is when a character struggles with his or her thoughts or emotions.

Major types of external conflicts include *man against nature*, *man against man*, and *man against society*. The man against nature conflict is
You can recognize conflicts in story plots by asking:
Who is the protagonist?
Who or what is the antagonist?
Why are the protagonist and antagonist in conflict?
What event(s) develop the conflict?
Which event is the climax?

## Transitions Words

Transition words can be helpful when writing a narrative so that readers can follow the events in a seamless manner. Sequence words such as *first*, *second*, and *last* assist readers in understanding the order in which events occur. Words such as *then* or *next* also show the order in which events occur. *After a while* and *before this* are other sequence expressions.

Additionally, transition words can indicate a change from one time frame or setting to another: "We were sitting on a rock near the lake when we heard a strange sound."At this point we decided to look to see where the noise was coming from by going further into the woods." In this excerpt the phrase *at this point* signals a shift in setting between what was happening and what came next.

## Precise Language

Your use of precise language, phrases, and sensory language (i.e., language that appeals to the five senses) helps readers imagine a place, situation, or person in the way that you intended. Details of character's actions, the setting, and the events in a narrative help create a lively and thought-provoking story. Sensory language helps convey the mood and feeling of the setting and characters and can highlight the theme of your story.

*Read the excerpt and analyze the language.*

> At dawn, in a stuffy and smoky second-class car in which five people had already spent the night, a bulky woman in deep mourning was hoisted in—almost like a shapeless bundle. Behind her, puffing and moaning, followed her husband—a tiny man, thin and weakly, his face death-white, his eyes small and bright and looking shy and uneasy.

The language selected by the author is filled with fresh and precise words that describe and color the two passengers as well as the setting of the paragraph. The author describes the car as *stuffy and smoky*, *second-class*, and *in which five people had already spent the night*. All this conjures up a dreary train car. The author describes the woman as *a shapeless bundle*. Her husband is *tiny*, *thin*, and *weakly* with a *death-white* face. These words give a clear image of what the people look like for readers which should be a goal of your creative writing.

## Role of a Conclusion

The conclusion of a narrative is extremely important because it shapes the entire story and is the resolution of the characters' conflict(s). Some conclusions may be tragic (e.g., classic tragedies), and other endings may be lighthearted (e.g., classic comedies). Modern stories tend to have endings that are more complex than the clear-cut endings of classic literature. They often leave readers without a clear sense of how a character fares at the end. Nonetheless, this element can show how life is not always clear in its conclusions.

*A student is writing a story about a boy who pushes himself to become an athlete. The student has written about how hard the boy has trained for an upcoming race. He has noted that winning has become a huge force in his life. Now, a conclusion is needed for the story. Describe what he should look for when he writes the conclusion.*

> The student should think about what the theme of the story is meant to be. Is it a story about someone who works hard and gets what he wants? Or is it about someone who

- 75 -

loses an important race and how he deals with it? Then, the student should carry that theme through to the ending of the story which in this case would be whether he won or lost the race. A conclusion should bring the entire story to an appropriate ending so that readers have a sense of closure.

**Traditional Essay Overview**

A traditional way to prepare for the writing section is to read. When you read newspapers, magazines, and books, you learn about new ideas. You can read newspapers and magazines to become informed about issues that affect many people.

As you think about those issues and ideas, you can take a position and form opinions. Try to develop these ideas and your opinions by sharing them with friends. After you develop your opinions, try writing them down as if you were going to spread your ideas beyond your friends.

For your exam you need to write an essay that shows your ability to understand and respond to an assignment. When you talk with others, you give beliefs, opinions, and ideas about the world around you. As you talk, you have the opportunity to share information with spoken words, facial expressions, or hand motions. If your audience seems confused about your ideas, you can stop and explain. However, when you write, you have a different assignment. As you write, you need to share information in a clear, precise way. Your readers will not have the chance to ask questions about your ideas. So, before you write your essay, you need to understand the assignment. As you write, you should be clear and precise about your ideas.

Brainstorm
Spend the first three to five minutes brainstorming for ideas. Write down any ideas that you might have on the topic. The purpose is to pull any helpful information from the depths of your memory. In this stage, anything goes down on note paper regardless of how good or bad the idea may seem at first glance. You may not bring your own paper for these notes. Instead, you will be provided with paper at the time of your test.

Strength through Different Viewpoints
The best papers will contain several examples and mature reasoning. As you brainstorm, you should consider different perspectives. There are more than two sides to every topic. In an argument, there are countless perspectives that can be considered. On any topic, different groups are impacted and many reach the same conclusion or position. Yet, they reach the same conclusion through different paths. Before writing your essay, try to *see* the topic through as many different *eyes* as you can.

Once you have finished with your creative flow, you need to stop and review what you brainstormed. *Which idea allowed you to come up with the most supporting information?* Be sure to pick an angle that will allow you to have a thorough coverage of the prompt.

Every garden of ideas has weeds. The ideas that you brainstormed are going to be random pieces of information of different values. Go through the pieces carefully and pick out the ones that are the best. The best ideas are strong points that will be easy to write a paragraph in response.

Now, you have your main ideas that you will focus on. So, align them in a sequence that will flow in a smooth, sensible path from point to point. With this approach, readers will go smoothly from one idea to the next in a reasonable order. Readers want an essay that has a sense of continuity (i.e., Point 1 to Point 2 to Point 3 and so on).

<u>Start Your Engines</u>
Now, you have a logical flow of the main ideas for the start of your essay. Begin by expanding on the first point, then move to your second point. Pace yourself. Don't spend too much time on any one of the ideas that you are expanding on. You want to have time for all of them. *Make sure that you watch your time.* If you have twenty minutes left to write out your ideas and you have four ideas, then you can only use five minutes per idea. Writing so much information in so little time can be an intimidating task. Yet, when you pace yourself, you can get through all of your points. If you find that you are falling behind, then you can remove one of your weaker arguments. This will allow you to give enough support to your remaining paragraphs.

Once you finish expanding on an idea, go back to your brainstorming session where you wrote out your ideas. You can scratch through the ideas as you write about them. This will let you see what you need to write about next and what you have left to cover.

Your introductory paragraph should have several easily identifiable features.

- First, the paragraph should have a quick description or paraphrasing of the topic. Use your own words to briefly explain what the topic is about.
- Second, you should list your writing points. What are the main ideas that you came up with earlier? If someone was to read only your introduction, they should be able to get a good summary of the entire paper.
- Third, you should explain your opinion of the topic and give an explanation for why you feel that way. What is your decision or conclusion on the topic?

Each of your following paragraphs should develop one of the points listed in the main paragraph. Use your personal experience and knowledge to support each of your points. Examples should back up everything.

Once you have finished expanding on each of your main points, you need to conclude your essay. Summarize what you written in a conclusion paragraph. Explain once more your argument on the prompt and review why you feel that way in a few sentences. At this stage, you have already backed up your statements. So, there is no need to do that again. You just need to refresh your readers on the main points that you made in your essay.

<u>Don't Panic</u>
Whatever you do during the essay, do not panic. When you panic, you will put fewer words on the page and your ideas will be weak. Therefore, panicking is not helpful. If your mind goes blank when you see the prompt, then you need to take a deep breath. Remember to brainstorm and put anything on scratch paper that comes to mind.

Also, don't get clock fever. You may be overwhelmed when you're looking at a page that is mostly blank. Your mind is full of random thoughts and feeling confused, and the clock is ticking down faster. You have already brainstormed for ideas. Therefore, you don't have to keep coming up with ideas. If you're running out of time and you have a lot of ideas that you haven't written down, then don't be afraid to make some cuts. Start picking the best ideas that you have left and expand on them. Don't feel like you have to write on all of your ideas.

A short paper that is well written and well organized is better than a long paper that is poorly written and poorly organized. Don't keep writing about a subject just to add sentences and avoid repeating a statement or idea that you have explained already. The goal is 1 to 2 pages of quality writing. That is your target, but you should not mess up your paper by trying to get there. You want to have a natural end to your work without having to cut something short. If your essay is a little long, then that isn't a problem as long as your ideas are clear and flow well from paragraph to paragraph. Just be sure that your writing stays inside the assigned borders of the papers. Remember to expand on the ideas that you identified in the brainstorming session.

Leave time at the end (at least three minutes) to go back and check over your work. Reread and make sure that everything you've written makes sense and flows well. Clean up any spelling or grammar mistakes. Also, go ahead and erase any brainstorming ideas that you weren't able to include. Then, clean up any extra information that you might have written that doesn't fit into your paper.

As you proofread, make sure that there aren't any fragments or run-ons. Check for sentences that are too short or too long. If the sentence is too short, then look to see if you have a specific subject and an active verb. If it is too long, then break up the long sentence into two sentences. Watch out for any "big words" that you may have used. Be sure that you are using difficult words correctly. Don't misunderstand; you should try to increase your vocabulary and use difficult words in your essay. However, your focus should be on developing and expressing ideas in a clear and precise way.

The Short Overview
Depending on your preferences and personality, the essay may be your hardest or your easiest section. You are required to go through the entire process of writing a paper in a limited amount of time which is very challenging.

Stay focused on each of the steps for brainstorming. Go through the process of creative flow first. You can start by generating ideas about the prompt. Next, organize those ideas into a smooth flow. Then, pick out the ideas that are the best from your list.

Create a recognizable essay structure in your paper. Start with an introduction that explains what you have decided to argue. Then, choose your main points. Use the body paragraphs to touch on those main points and have a conclusion that wraps up the topic.

Save a few moments to go back and review what you have written. Clean up any minor mistakes that you might have made and make those last few critical touches that can make a huge difference. Finally, be proud and confident of what you have written!

# Writing

*Review the following prompts and choose to write a creative story or a traditional essay. You have 25 minutes to write a creative story or respond to the traditional essay prompt.*

<u>Creative Writing</u>
"I learned that courage was not the absence of fear, but the triumph over it. The brave man is not he who does not feel afraid, but he who conquers that fear."
-Nelson Mandela

Think carefully about this quote and the difference that having courage makes. Then, write a creative story that covers the importance of exercising courage in everyday life.

<u>Essay Writing</u>
Prompt: NSA wiretapping and spying policies have been a topic of interest lately with much discussion taking place over the need for security as it relates to the right to individual privacy.

Write an essay that takes a position on whether you support or oppose government collection of private data for the purpose of national security. Use arguments and examples to support your position.

# Section 1: Quantitative

1. Janice makes $x$ phone calls. Elaina makes 23 more phone calls than Janice. June makes 14 more phone calls than Janice. In terms of $x$, what is the sum of their phone calls minus 25 calls?

    a. 3x + 37
    b. 3x + 12
    c. x + 12
    d. 3x - 25
    e. 9x - 25

2. Olga drew the regular figure shown here. She painted part of the figure a light color and part of it a darker color. She left the rest of the figure white.

Which of the following equations best models the part of the figure Olga left white?

    a. $1 - \frac{1}{3} - \frac{1}{3} = \frac{1}{3}$

    b. $1 - \frac{1}{6} - \frac{1}{6} = \frac{2}{3}$

    c. $1 - \frac{1}{6} - \frac{1}{2} = \frac{1}{3}$

    d. $1 - \frac{1}{2} - \frac{1}{3} = \frac{2}{3}$

    e. $1 - \frac{1}{2} - \frac{1}{6} = \frac{2}{3}$

3. On a floor plan drawn at a scale of 1:100, the area of a rectangular room is 30 cm$^2$. What is the actual area of the room?

    a. 30 m$^2$
    b. 300 cm$^2$
    c. 300 m$^2$
    d. 3,000 m$^2$
    e. 30,000 cm$^2$

4. Restaurant customers tip their server only 8 percent for poor service. If their tip was $4, how much was their bill?

    a. $40
    b. $42
    c. $46
    d. $48
    e. $50

5. The number of flights a flight attendant made per month is represented by the line graph below.

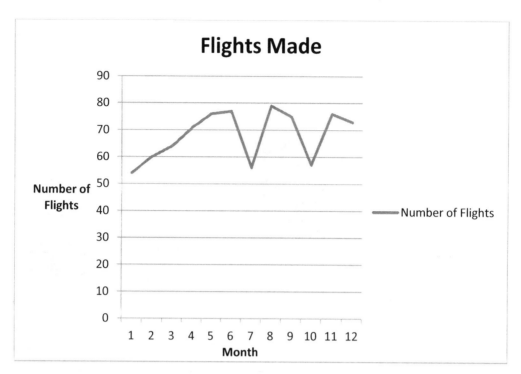

What is the range in the number of flights the flight attendant made?
    a. 20
    b. 22
    c. 25
    d. 29
    e. 32

6. In Figure 1 (pictured below), the distance from $A$ to $D$ is 48. The distance from $A$ to $B$ is equal to the distance from $B$ to $C$. If the distance from $C$ to $D$ is twice the distance of $A$ to $B$, how far apart are $B$ and $D$?
    a. 12
    b. 16
    c. 19
    d. 24
    e. 36

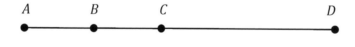

Figure 1

7. John buys 100 shares of stock at $100 per share. The price goes up by 10% and he sells 50 shares. Then, prices drop by 10% and he sells his remaining 50 shares. How much did he get for the last 50?
    a. $4000
    b. $4900
    c. $4950
    d. $5000
    e. $5500

8. A long distance runner does a first lap around a track in exactly 50 seconds. As she tires, each subsequent lap takes 20% longer than the previous one. How long does she take to run 3 laps?
    a. 72 seconds
    b. 160 seconds
    c. 180 seconds
    d. 182 seconds
    e. 190 seconds

9. Hannah draws two supplementary angles. One angle measures 34°. What is the measure of the other angle?
    a. 56°
    b. 66°
    c. 146°
    d. 168°
    e. 326°

10. Jeremy put a heavy chalk mark on the tire of his bicycle. His bike tire is 27 inches in diameter. When he rolled the bike, the chalk left marks on the sidewalk. Which expression can be used to best determine the distance, in inches, the bike rolled from the first mark to the fourth mark?
    a. $3(27\pi)$
    b. $4\pi(27)$
    c. $(27 \div 3)\pi$
    d. $(27 \div 4)\pi$
    e. $4\pi(27 \div 3)$

11. A data set has five values: 5, 10, 12, 13, and one unknown value. The average of the data set is 9.6. What is the unknown value?
    a. 4.6
    b. 5
    c. 6
    d. 7.2
    e. 8

12. A hat contains 6 red dice, 4 green dice, and 2 blue dice. What is the probability that Sarah pulls out a blue die, replaces it, and then pulls out a green die?

    a. $\dfrac{1}{18}$

    b. $\dfrac{1}{16}$

    c. $\dfrac{2}{12}$

    d. $\dfrac{1}{3}$

    e. $\dfrac{1}{2}$

13. If $a - 16 = 8b + 6$, what does $a + 3$ equal?

    a. b + 3

    b. 8b + 9

    c. 8b + 22

    d. 8b + 25

    e. b + 6

14. A bag of coffee costs $9.85 and contains 16 ounces of coffee. Which of the following best represents the cost per ounce?

    a. $0.62

    b. $0.64

    c. $0.65

    d. $0.67

    e. $0.70

15. What is the slope of the line shown in the graph?

    a. 7

    b. 14

    c. 16

    d. 21

    e. 28

16. Adam builds a bridge that is 12 feet long. If 1 foot equals 0.3048 meters, which of the following best represents the length of the bridge, in meters?
    a. 1.83 meters
    b. 3.66 meters
    c. 4.96 meters
    d. 5.7 meters
    e. 39.37 meters

17. Amy saves $450 every 3 months. How much does she save after 3 years?
    a. $4,800
    b. $5,200
    c. $5,400
    d. $5,800
    e. $6,000

18. The figure below shows a square. If side AD = 10 and if AE = EB and BF = FC, what is the area of the shaded region?

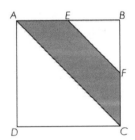

    a. 16.5
    b. 24
    c. 28
    d. 37.5
    e. 42.5

19. Simplify the following equation: $4(6 - 3)^2 - (-2)$
    a. 34
    b. 36
    c. 38
    d. 42
    e. 48

20. If $\sqrt{x} - 2 = 8$, determine the value of $x$.
    a. 64
    b. 66
    c. 100
    d. 110
    e. 144

21. Which of the following transformations has been applied to $\triangle ABC$?

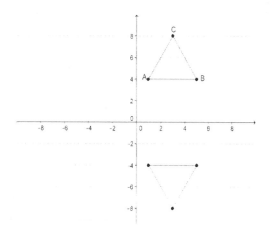

    a. translation
    b. rotation of 90 degrees
    c. reflection
    d. dilation
    e. rotation of 180 degrees

22. The distance between two towns is 275 miles. A truck driver must leave one town and arrive at the other at 9:30 p.m. If the trucker drives at an average rate of 55 miles per hour, at what time should the trucker depart?
    a. 4:00 p.m.
    b. 4:30 p.m.
    c. 5:00 p.m.
    d. 4:00 a.m.
    e. 4:30 a.m.

23. The chart below shows the annual number of visitors to the Augusta Planetarium. Which year shows the greatest increase in visitors over the prior year?

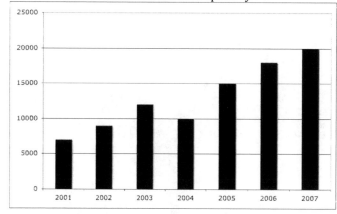

    a. 2001
    b. 2002
    c. 2003
    d. 2004
    e. 2005

24. What is the simplest way to write the following expression?
5x – 2y + 4x + y

    a. 9x – y
    b. 9x – 3y
    c. 9x + 3y
    d. x ; y
    e. 9x + y

25. A wall clock has the numbers 1 through 12 written on it. If you spin the second hand, what is the probability of landing on an even number?

    a. 10%
    b. 20%
    c. 30%
    d. 40%
    e. 50%

# Section 2: Reading Comprehension

## Global Warming

Global warming and the depletion of natural resources are constant threats to the future of our planet. All people have a responsibility to be proactive participants in the fight to save Earth by working now to conserve resources for later. Participation begins with our everyday choices. From what you buy to what you do to how much you use, your decisions affect the planet and everyone around you. Now is the time to take action.

When choosing what to buy, look for sustainable products made from renewable or recycled resources. The packaging of the products you buy is just as important as the products themselves. Is the item minimally packaged in a recycled container? How did the product reach the store? Locally grown food and other products manufactured within your community are the best choices. The fewer miles a product traveled to reach you, the fewer resources it required.

You can continue to make a difference for the planet in how you use what you bought and the resources you have available. Remember the locally grown food you purchased? Don't pile it on your plate at dinner. Food that remains on your plate is a wasted resource, and you can always go back for seconds. You should try to be aware of your consumption of water and energy. Turn off the water when you brush your teeth, and limit your showers to five minutes. Turn off the lights, and don't leave appliances or chargers plugged in when not in use.

Together, we can use less, waste less, recycle more, and make the right choices. It may be the only chance we have.

1. What is the author's primary purpose in writing this article?
    a. The author's purpose is to scare people.
    b. The author's purpose is to warn people.
    c. The author's purpose is to inspire people.
    d. The author's purpose is to inform people.
    e. The author's purpose is to scold people.

2. How does the author make a connection between the second and third paragraphs (lines 7-19)?
    a. The author indicates he will now make suggestions for how to use what you bought.
    b. The author indicates he will continue to give more examples of what you should buy.
    c. The author indicates he will make suggestions for how to keep from buying more items.
    d. The author indicates he will make suggestions for how to tell other people what to buy.
    e. The author indicates he will continue to encourage people to be aware of their energy consumption.

3. What is the main idea of this article?
   a. People should use less water and energy.
   b. People should make responsible choices in what they purchase and how they use their available resources.
   c. People are quickly destroying the earth, and there is no way to stop the destruction.
   d. People should organize everyone they know to join the fight to save the environment.
   e. A few people need to keep the majority encouraged to save the planet's resources.

4. Which organizational pattern did the author use?
   a. Comparison and contrast
   b. Chronological order
   c. Cause and effect
   d. Problem/solution
   e. None of the above

5. What does the author say is the place to begin saving our planet?
   a. The place to begin is with getting rid of products that are not earth friendly.
   b. The place to begin is with using less water when we take a shower.
   c. The place to begin is with a commitment to fight for the improvement of Earth.
   d. The place to begin is with buying locally-grown food.
   e. The place to begin is with the choices we make every day.

6. What does the author imply will happen if people do not follow his suggestions?
   a. The author implies we will run out of resources in the next 10 years.
   b. The author implies water and energy prices will rise sharply in the near future.
   c. The author implies global warming and the depletion of natural resources will continue.
   d. The author implies local farmers will lose their farms.
   e. The author implies that we will other opportunities to save the planet.

## The Educational Market Town

Aberystwyth is a market town on the West Coast of Wales within the United Kingdom. A market town refers to European areas that have the right to have markets, which differentiates it from a city or village. The town is located where two rivers meet, the River Ystwyth and River Rheidol and is best known as an educational center, housing an established university since 1872.

The town is situated between North Wales and South Wales, and is a large vacation destination as well as a tourist attraction. Constitution Hill is a hill on the north end of Aberystwyth, which provides excellent views of Cardigan Bay and which is supported by the Aberystwyth Electric Cliff Railway. Although Aberystwyth is known as a modern Welsh town, it is home to several historic buildings, such as the remnants of a castle.

Although there are several grocery, clothing, sporting goods, and various other miscellaneous shops, Aberystwyth is best known for its educational services. Aberystwyth University, formerly known as University College Wales, as well as the National Library of Wales, which is the legal deposit library for Wales and which houses all Welsh publications, are both located within Aberystwyth. The two main languages traditionally spoken in Aberystwyth are English and Welsh. With local live music, arts center, and educational opportunities in gorgeous scenery, Aberystwyth is a hidden luxury within the United Kingdom.

7. Where is Aberystwyth located?
    a. England
    b. Ireland
    c. Scotland
    d. Wales
    e. Isle of Man

8. What is the purpose of this essay?
    a. To explain that the university was established in 1872
    b. To explain the legal deposit library in Wales
    c. To provide a portrait of a town
    d. To explain the views in Aberystwyth
    e. To help tourists

9. What does the word *situated* mean in paragraph 2?
    a. located
    b. fighting
    c. luxurious
    d. hidden
    e. indefinite

10. Which of the following statements is an opinion?
    a. Although Aberystwyth is known as a modern Welsh town, it is home to several historic buildings, such as the remnants of a castle
    b. With local live music, arts center, and educational opportunities in gorgeous scenery, Aberystwyth is a hidden luxury within the United Kingdom
    c. The two main languages traditionally spoken in Aberystwyth are English and Welsh
    d. Aberystwyth is a market town on the West Coast of Wales within the United Kingdom
    e. Aberystwyth is best known for its educational services

11. How many languages are traditionally spoken in Aberystwyth?
    a. One
    b. Two
    c. Three
    d. Four
    e. More than four

12. What makes Aberystwyth a market town?
    a. It is a city
    b. It is a village
    c. It has the right to have a market
    d. There are markets in town every day
    e. The local live music, arts center, and educational opportunities

13. What is Constitution Hill supported by?
    a. Cardigan Bay
    b. The ocean
    c. North Wales
    d. Aberystwyth Electric Cliff Railway
    e. Tourism

14. What is Aberystwyth best known as?
    a. An educational center
    b. A market town
    c. A music center
    d. A hiking center
    e. A large vacation destination

### An Excerpt from <u>The Fifty-First Dragon</u> by Heywood Broun

Of all the pupils at the knight school Gawaine le Cœur-Hardy was among the least promising. He was tall and sturdy, but his instructors soon discovered that he lacked spirit. He would hide in the woods when the jousting class was called, although his companions and members of the faculty sought to appeal to his better nature by shouting to him to come out and break his neck like a man. Even when they told him that the lances were padded, the horses no more than ponies and the field unusually soft for late autumn, Gawaine refused to grow enthusiastic. The Headmaster and the Assistant Professor of Pleasaunce were discussing the case one spring afternoon and the Assistant Professor could see no remedy but expulsion.

"No," said the Headmaster, as he looked out at the purple hills which ringed the school, "I think I'll train him to slay dragons."

"He might be killed," objected the Assistant Professor.

"So he might," replied the Headmaster brightly, but he added, more soberly, "we must consider the greater good. We are responsible for the formation of this lad's character."

"Are the dragons particularly bad this year?" interrupted the Assistant Professor. This was characteristic. He always seemed restive when the head of the school began to talk ethics and the ideals of the institution.

"I've never known them worse," replied the Headmaster. "Up in the hills to the south last week they killed a number of peasants, two cows and a prize pig. And if this dry spell holds there's no telling when they may start a forest fire simply by breathing around indiscriminately."

"Would any refund on the tuition fee be necessary in case of an accident to young Cœur-Hardy?"

"No," the principal answered, judicially, "that's all covered in the contract. But as a matter of fact he won't be killed. Before I send him up in the hills I'm going to give him a magic word."

"That's a good idea," said the Professor. "Sometimes they work wonders."

15. What is this passage about?
    a. The problems that may arise from fighting dragons
    b. How the educators would change Gawaine's course of study
    c. The way the Professor and the Headmaster taught about dragons
    d. Giving Gawaine a magic word to help him fight dragons
    e. A shy boy's troubles in a new school environment

16. What can be inferred about Gawaine le Couer-Hardy from the first paragraph (lines 1-9)?
    a. Gawaine does not want to be a knight
    b. Gawaine is not as strong as the other pupils at the knight school
    c. Gawaine's family history is made of unremarkable knights
    d. Gawaine enjoys playing in the forest
    e. Gawaine has no friends at the school

17. What is the best way to describe Gawaine's character?
    a. Fearless and excitable
    b. Careless and frigid
    c. Spiritual and careful
    d. Cowardly and apathetic
    e. Rebellious and misunderstood

18. What is the meaning of "his better nature"?
    a. An increased sense of honesty
    b. Gawaine's love interest
    c. A desire for ownership
    d. A man's nobler instincts
    e. His knowledge of the forests

19. Why does the Headmaster mention some "peasants, two cows, and a prize pig"?
    a. To help the professor understand dragon behavior
    b. To show that Gawaine would be perfect for fighting dragons
    c. To illustrate how much trouble dragons are this year
    d. To explain why Gawaine's talents were needed
    e. To remind the professor of the painful event

20. How does the Headmaster put the professor at ease about Gawaine?
    a. He tells him that Gawaine will only fight small dragons.
    b. He assures him that Gawaine's contract has not expired.
    c. He talks to him about the animals that have been killed by the dragons.
    d. He reminds him of their responsibility for the boy's character.
    e. He mentions that Gawaine will be given a magic word.

### Charles Darwin on the Galapagos Islands

During the 1800s, Charles Darwin became known for his studies of plants and animals on the Galapagos Islands. He is often referred to as "the father of evolution," because he was first to describe a mechanism by which organisms change over time.

The Galapagos Islands are situated off the coast of South America. Much of Darwin's work on the islands focused on the birds. He noticed that island birds looked similar to finches on the South American continent and resembled a type of modified finch. The only differences in the finches Darwin saw were in their beaks and the kind of food they ate. Finches on the mainland were seed-eating birds, but the island finches ate insects, seeds, plant matter, egg yolks, and blood.

Darwin theorized that the island finches were offspring of one type of mainland finch. The population of finches was changing over time due to their environment. He believed the finches' eating habits changed because of the island's limited food supply. As the finches began to eat differently, the way their beaks worked and looked changed as well. For instance, insect-eating finches needed longer beaks for digging in the ground. Seed-eating and nut-eating finches required thicker beaks to crack the seed shells.

The process by which the finches changed happened over many generations. Among the population of beetle-eating finches, those finches born with longer, sharper beaks naturally had access to more beetles than those finches with shorter beaks. As a result, the sharp-beaked, insect-eating finches thrived and produced many offspring, while the short-beaked insect-eating finches gradually died out. The sharp beak was in effect selected by nature to thrive. The same thing happened in each finch population until finches within the same population began to look similar to each other and different from finches of other populations. These observations eventually led Darwin to develop the theory of natural selection.

21. Why is Charles Darwin called "the father of evolution"?
    a. because he coined the term "evolution"
    b. because he was the first scientist to study species on the Galapagos Islands
    c. because he was the first to describe how organisms changed over time
    d. because he was the first to suggest that birds adapted to their environment
    e. because he was the first to develop the theory of natural selection

22. What is the main point of this passage?
    a. to inform
    b. to entertain
    c. to critique
    d. to persuade
    e. to shock

23. According to the passage, why did finches with sharp, long beaks thrive while other finches died off?
    a. They were able to reproduce faster than other types of finches on the island.
    b. They were more numerous and eventually outlived the other finches on the island.
    c. They were randomly selected by nature to reproduce over other types of finches on the island.
    d. They had a diet that improved their fitness for their environment
    e. They had better access to insects than other types of finches on the island.

24. Based on Darwin's studies on the islands, what could also be inferred about how geography affects the diversity of species?
   a. Geographical barriers decrease diversity of a species.
   b. Geographical barriers increase diversity of a species.
   c. Geographical barriers have an insignificant impact on the diversity of a species.
   d. Geographical barriers left the finches open to predators
   e. There is no relationship between geographical barriers and the diversity of a species.

25. Which of the following statements correctly compares the finches Darwin observed in the Galapagos Islands with the finches found on the mainland?
   a. The island finches were very similar with no visible differences.
   b. The island finches differed only in the shape of their beaks.
   c. The island finches differed only in size.
   d. The island finches differed in the shape of their beaks and their diet.
   e. The island finches produced fewer offspring.

## New Zealand Inhabitants

The islands of New Zealand are among the most remote of all the Pacific islands. New Zealand is an archipelago, with two large islands and a number of smaller ones. Its climate is far cooler than the rest of Polynesia. Nevertheless, according to Maori legends, it was colonized in the early fifteenth century by a wave of Polynesian voyagers who traveled southward in their canoes and settled on North Island. At this time, New Zealand was already known to the Polynesians, who had probably first landed there some 400 years earlier.

The Polynesian southward migration was limited by the availability of food. Traditional Polynesian tropical crops such as taro and yams will grow on North Island, but the climate of South Island is too cold for them. Coconuts will not grow on either island. The first settlers were forced to rely on hunting and gathering, and, of course, fishing. Especially on South Island, most settlements remained close to the sea. At the time of the Polynesian influx, enormous flocks of moa birds had their rookeries on the island shores. These flightless birds were easy prey for the settlers, and within a few centuries had been hunted to extinction. Fish, shellfish and the roots of the fern were other important sources of food, but even these began to diminish in quantity as the human population increased. The Maori had few other sources of meat: dogs, smaller birds, and rats. Archaeological evidence shows that human flesh was also eaten, and that tribal warfare increased markedly after the moa disappeared.

By far the most important farmed crop in prehistoric New Zealand was the sweet potato. This tuber is hearty enough to grow throughout the islands, and could be stored to provide food during the winter months, when other food-gathering activities were difficult. The availability of the sweet potato made possible a significant increase in the human population. Maori tribes often lived in encampments called *pa*, which were fortified with earthen embankments and usually located near the best sweet potato farmlands.

26. A definition for the word *archipelago* is
    a. A country
    b. A place in the southern hemisphere
    c. A group of islands
    d. A roosting place for birds
    e. A place with few visitors

27. This article is primarily about what?
    a. The geology of New Zealand
    b. New Zealand's early history
    c. New Zealand's prehistory
    d. Food sources used by New Zealand's first colonists
    e. The differences between the North Island and the South Island

28. Why did early settlements remain close to the sea?
    a. The people liked to swim
    b. The people didn't want to get far from the boats they had come in
    c. Taro and yams grow only close to the beaches
    d. They were dependent upon sea creatures for their food
    e. They would be able to leave the island quickly if they were attacked

29. Why do you suppose tribal warfare increased after the moa disappeared?
    a. Increased competition for food led the people to fight
    b. Some groups blamed others for the moa's extinction
    c. They had more time on their hands since they couldn't hunt the moa, so they fought
    d. One group was trying to consolidate political control over the entire country
    e. None of the above

30. How did the colder weather of New Zealand make it difficult for the Polynesians to live there?
    a. The Polynesians weren't used to making warm clothes
    b. Cold water fish are harder to catch
    c. Some of them froze
    d. Some of their traditional crops would not grow there
    e. They had to use too many resources to make their shelters

31. Why was it important that sweet potatoes could be stored?
    a. They could be eaten in winter, when other foods were scarce
    b. They could be traded for fish and other goods
    c. They could be taken along by groups of warriors going to war
    d. They tasted better after a few weeks of storage
    e. It allowed farmers to use more space for other foods

## "The Road Not Taken" by Robert Frost

Two roads diverged in a yellow wood,
And sorry I could not travel both
And be one traveler, long I stood
And looked down one as far as I could
To where it bent in the undergrowth;

Then took the other, as just as fair,
And having perhaps the better claim,
Because it was grassy and wanted wear;
Though as for that the passing there
Had worn them really about the same,

And both that morning equally lay
In leaves no step had trodden black.
Oh, I kept the first for another day!
Yet knowing how way leads on to way,
I doubted if I should ever come back.
I shall be telling this with a sigh
Somewhere ages and ages hence:
Two roads diverged in a wood, and I—
I took the one less traveled by,
And that has made all the difference.

32. In the second stanza, is there a big difference between one road and the other?
    a. Yes, because one path is more dangerous than the other.
    b. Yes, because one road is much less traveled than the other.
    c. No, because one road is only a little less traveled than the other.
    d. No, because both roads lead to the same place in the end.
    e. There is not enough information given to the reader to make a decision.

33. Why does the narrator of the poem say that he will tell the story of the two roads "With a sigh/ Somewhere ages and ages hence"?
    a. The narrator is regretting the choice he has made.
    b. The narrator is sad that he had to walk alone.
    c. The narrator is looking back on a fond memory.
    d. The narrator does not remember what happened.
    e. The narrator knows that the two roads were removed many years ago

34. Why is the path in the middle of the woods, rather than a road through the city?
    a. There are no signs to point out which road is faster.
    b. There are no distractions from the decision that the narrator has to make.
    c. There are no other people who can give the narrator advice.
    d. All of the above
    e. None of the above

35. Why does the narrator of the poem take so long to make a decision?
   a. He is not sure where the roads will lead him.
   b. He is trying to guess which road will be best for exploring.
   c. He is trying to remember if he has walked this way before.
   d. He is sure that one of the choices will be a wrong turn.
   e. He thinks the choice he makes represents who he is.

36. What does it say about the narrator that he wants to take the road less traveled?
   a. He wants to explore a place that no one has ever been to before.
   b. He wants to feel unique by making a less popular journey.
   c. He wants to take a shortcut through the woods.
   d. He wants to avoid other people.
   e. He wants to show off his bravery to other people.

## The Inventions of Technology

Stories have been a part of the world since the beginning of recorded time. For centuries before the invention of the printing press, stories of the world were passed down to generations through oral tradition. With the invention of the printing press, which made written material available to wide ranges of audiences, books were mass-produced and introduced into greater society.

For the last several centuries, books have been at the forefront of education and entertainment. With the invention of the Internet, reliance on books for information quickly changed. Soon, almost everything that anyone needed to know could be accessed through the Internet. Large printed volumes of encyclopedias became unnecessary as all of the information was easily available on the Internet.

Despite the progression of the Internet, printed media was still very popular in the forms of both fiction and non-fiction books. While waiting for an appointment, enduring a several-hour flight, or relaxing before sleep, books have been a reliable and convenient source of entertainment, and one that society has not been willing to give up.

With the progression and extreme convenience of technology, printed books are going to soon become a thing of the past. Inventions such as the iPad from Macintosh and the Kindle have made the need for any kind of printed media unnecessary. With a rechargeable battery, a large screen, and the ability to have several books saved on file, electronic options will soon take over and society will no longer see printed books.

Although some people may say that the act of reading is not complete without turning a page, sliding a finger across the screen or pressing a button to read more onto the next page is just as satisfying to the reader. The iPad and Kindle are devices that have qualities similar to a computer and can be used for so much more than just reading. These devices are therefore better than books because they have multiple uses.

In a cultural society that is part of the world and due to a longstanding tradition, stories will always be an important way to communicate ideas and provide information and entertainment. Centuries ago, stories could only be remembered and retold through speech. Printed media changed the way the world communicated and was connected, and now, as we move forward with technology, it is only a matter of time before we must say goodbye to the printed past and welcome the digital and electronic future.

37. What is the main argument of this essay?
   a. iPad and Kindles are easier to read than books
   b. The printing press was a great invention
   c. The Internet is how people receive information
   d. Technology will soon replace printed material
   e. People need frequent changes in how they receive stories

38. What is the main purpose of paragraph 1?
   a. To explain oral tradition
   b. To explain the importance of the printing press
   c. To explain the progression of stories within society
   d. To introduce the essay
   e. To show why iPads and Kindles are necessary today

39. According to the essay, what was the first way that stories were communicated and passed down?
   a. Oral tradition
   b. Printed books
   c. Technology
   d. Hand writing
   e. Cave drawings

40. Which of the following statements is an opinion?
   a. Despite the progression of the Internet, printed media was still very popular in the forms of both fiction and non-fiction books.
   b. The iPad and Kindle are devices that have qualities similar to a computer and can be used for so much more than just reading.
   c. With the invention of the Internet, reliance on books for information quickly changed.
   d. Stories have been a part of the world since the beginning of recorded time.
   e. Although some people may say that the act of reading is not complete without turning a page, sliding a finger across the screen or pressing a button to read more onto the next page is just as satisfying to the reader.

## Section 3: Verbal

### Synonyms

*Directions: Select the one word whose meaning is closest to the word in capital letters.*

1. ABROAD
    a. harsh
    b. overseas
    c. selfish
    d. truthful
    e. reception

2. RUMINATE
    a. concern
    b. decision
    c. hesitation
    d. reflect
    e. neglect

3. CONCISE
    a. brief
    b. difficult
    c. lengthy
    d. reasonable
    e. repetitive

4. MOURN
    a. cry
    b. direction
    c. approve
    d. help
    e. praise

5. RESIDENCE
    a. home
    b. area
    c. office
    d. resist
    e. warehouse

6. LEVITY
    a. attended
    b. delivered
    c. happiness
    d. prepared
    e. serious

7. RASH
   a. wise
   b. careless
   c. plan
   d. shy
   e. event

8. BANISH
   a. experiences
   b. pleasures
   c. remove
   d. solutions
   e. welcome

9. OPPORTUNITY
   a. direction
   b. chance
   c. conclusion
   d. caution
   e. sequence

10. DISABLE
   a. improve
   b. lecture
   c. rebuke
   d. replace
   e. damage

11. FRAGILE
   a. reliable
   b. firm
   c. constant
   d. delicate
   e. healthy

12. LOYAL
   a. cover
   b. proof
   c. calm
   d. faithful
   e. healthy

13. PRINCIPLE
   a. end
   b. overall
   c. punctual
   d. standard
   e. uncertain

14. ASSESS
    a. anger
    b. ignore
    c. determine
    d. loneliness
    e. guess

15. MORAL
    a. arrive
    b. fake
    c. honest
    d. portion
    e. unfair

16. SUPERIOR
    a. short
    b. similar
    c. better
    d. weak
    e. usual

17. REMARK
    a. rebuke
    b. comment
    c. lecture
    d. replace
    e. question

18. SPECIFY
    a. confuse
    b. indicate
    c. solid
    d. sturdy
    e. unsettle

19. COMMENCE
    a. begin
    b. progress
    c. finish
    d. comment
    e. exhaust

20. SWIFTLY
    a. surely
    b. quickly
    c. slowly
    d. lightly
    e. lazy

21. WILY
    a. clever
    b. dainty
    c. open
    d. trustworthy
    e. direct

22. HUMANE
    a. cold
    b. fed
    c. friendly
    d. hunted
    e. selfish

23. ASSERT
    a. deny
    b. argue
    c. hesitate
    d. perform
    e. surrender

24. PERILOUS
    a. normal
    b. secure
    c. emblem
    d. guarded
    e. hazardous

25. DONATE
    a. interrupt
    b. excessive
    c. contribute
    d. petition
    e. reserve

26. FINITE
    a. described
    b. intended
    c. limited
    d. wanted
    e. endless

27. DOCILE
    a. disagree
    b. obedient
    c. relate
    d. state
    e. determined

28. TAINT
    a. built
    b. clean
    c. damage
    d. improve
    e. unite

29. FALTER
    a. criticism
    b. delivery
    c. statement
    d. stumble
    e. steady

30. ABRUPTLY
    a. commonly
    b. homely
    c. slowly
    d. suddenly
    e. gradually

# Analogies

*Directions: For each of the following questions, you will find terms and five answer choices designated a, b, c, d, and e. Select the one answer choice that best completes the analogy.*

31. Historian is to perspective as
    a. explorer is to questionable
    b. victim is to autopsy
    c. native is to insight
    d. fact is to opinion
    e. director is to spirit

32. Geography is to mountains as history is to
    a. preserved
    b. events
    c. roots
    d. future
    e. behavior

33. Exhale is to inhale as
    a. annual is to yearly
    b. reckless is to brave
    c. spontaneous is to chaos
    d. invert is to reverse
    e. consent is to prohibit

34. Fiction is to myth as nonfiction is to
    a. drama
    b. poem
    c. legend
    d. biography
    e. hero

35. Astronomer is to encounter as
    a. vendor is to protect
    b. commander is to resign
    c. prophet is to inform
    d. academic is to camouflage
    e. architect is to disorient

36. Dual is to duel as
    a. docile is to fossil
    b. seam is to seem
    c. factor is to feature
    d. finite is to ample
    e. twice is to double

37. Nausea is to illness as
    a. bacteria is to infection
    b. surgery is to fracture
    c. frail is to vulnerable
    d. disease is to potent
    e. pollen is to flower

38. Evidence is to condemn
    a. generator is to restore
    b. gauge is to dignity
    c. antidote is to tension
    d. destruction is to chariot
    e. preamble is to threat

39. Liberty is to freedom as faithful is to
    a. triumph
    b. nimble
    c. sincere
    d. advantage
    e. inspect

40. Masculine is to feminine as
    a. paternal is to dad
    b. invincible is to undefeatable
    c. community is to individual
    d. defiant is to resistant
    e. concise is to summary

41. Artist is to imagination as advisor is to
    a. despair
    b. clarity
    c. oppress
    d. regal
    e. renew

42. Temple is to sacred as
    a. furnace is to basement
    b. auditorium is to musical
    c. church is to member
    d. sanctuary is to lofty
    e. cocoon is to violent

43. Gourmet is to critic as
    a. menu is to diverse
    b. meager is to portion
    c. cuisine is to exotic
    d. brick is to mason
    e. spice is to ingredient

44. Summit is to mountain as king is to
    a. battlefield
    b. powerful
    c. monarchy
    d. liberator
    e. parliament

45. Tactics is to marine
    a. data is to researcher
    b. navigate is to inspector
    c. forecast is to conductor
    d. distract is to editor
    e. incompetent is to trader

46. Chamber is to contain as
    a. throne is to cower
    b. agenda is to organize
    c. nook is to comfort
    d. chronicle is to story
    e. banjo is to instrument

47. Altar is to alter as
    a. loom is to whom
    b. shrine is to change
    c. denial is to veto
    d. rain is to reign
    e. align is to adjust

48. Nutrition is to physician as
    a. refugee is to nomad
    b. wildlife is to guide
    c. pottery is to navigator
    d. pitfall is to colonist
    e. tyranny is to tourist

49. Bravery is to cowardice as comedy is to
    a. glee
    b. grief
    c. celebrate
    d. relief
    e. inspire

50. Child is to naive as
    a. novice is to wisdom
    b. medal is to exhibit
    c. mother is to censor
    d. baptism is to custom
    e. soldier is to disciplined

51. Colonel is to kernel as
    a. agile is to fragile
    b. serial is to cereal
    c. mantle is to dismantle
    d. concept is to sonnet
    e. imply is to ally

52. Proton is to electron as
    a. productive is to efficient
    b. wept is to mourn
    c. renewable is to energy
    d. potent is to ineffective
    e. chromosome is to neutron

53. Documentary is to protestor as
    a. persist is to director
    b. banished is to renegade
    c. unpopular is to resident
    d. rotor is to mechanic
    e. fashion is to patriot

54. Tear is to tier as air is to
    a. breath
    b. ozone
    c. heir
    d. dare
    e. spare

55. Epidemic is to plague as vigor is to
   a. pneumonia
   b. endurance
   c. incompetence
   d. apathy
   e. postseason

56. Eternal is to momentary as
   a. frequent is to periodic
   b. express is to rash
   c. hinder is to interfere
   d. exotic is to ordinary
   e. termination is to decline

57. Meadow is to tranquility as
   a. tributary is to consoling
   b. suburbs is to danger
   c. prairie is to campfire
   d. traffic is to boring
   e. exercise is to rural

58. Verses is to versus as
   a. autobiography is to competition
   b. lane is to cane
   c. receive is to recieve
   d. carat is to carrot
   e. poetry is to confront

59. Aviator is to destination as sculptor is to
   a. originals
   b. restore
   c. unrest
   d. cathedral
   e. strategy

60. Constellation is to star as
   a. president is to campaign
   b. child is to prank
   c. sprout is to bloom
   d. movement is to locomotive
   e. orchestra is to instrument

# Section 4: Quantitative

1. How many one-fourths are contained in $8\frac{1}{2}$?
   a. 17
   b. 34
   c. 36
   d. 42
   e. 64

2. Given the sequence represented in the table below, where $n$ represents the position of the term and $a_n$ represents the value of the term, which of the following describes the relationship between the position number and the value of the term?

| $n$ | 1 | 2 | 3 | 4 | 5 | 6 |
|-----|---|---|----|----|----|-----|
| $a_n$ | 5 | 2 | −1 | −4 | −7 | −10 |

   a. Multiply $n$ by 2 and subtract 4
   b. Multiply $n$ by 2 and subtract 3
   c. Multiply $n$ by −3 and add 8
   d. Multiply $n$ by −4 and add 1
   e. Multiply $n$ by −3 and subtract 8

3. A triangle has the following angle measures: 98°, 47°, and 35°. What type of triangle is it?
   a. equidistant
   b. right
   c. equiangular
   d. acute
   e. obtuse

4. The TV weatherman warned of a snowstorm approaching the area. If the snow is supposed to fall at a rate of 2 inches per hour, which of the following equations represents the total snowfall ($t$) after it has been snowing for $h$ hours?
   a. $t = \frac{2}{h}$
   b. $t = h + 2$
   c. $t = h - 2$
   d. $t = 2h$
   e. $t = 2 - h$

5. Student scores on Mrs. Thompson's last math test are shown below. Which of the following is the best representation of class performance?
   $$76, 39, 87, 85, 91, 93, 86, 90, 77, 89, 74, 82, 68, 86, 79$$
   a. mean
   b. median
   c. mode
   d. range
   e. None of the above

6. In the figure below, find the value of *x*:

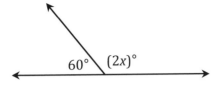

    a. 30
    b. 60
    c. 80
    d. 100
    e. 120

7. If number *x* is subtracted from 27, the result is -5. What is number *x*?
    a. 19
    b. 22
    c. 23
    d. 25
    e. 32

8. Which of the following is equivalent to $4^3 + 12 \div 4 + 8^2 \times 3$?
    a. 211
    b. 249
    c. 259
    d. 278
    e. 393

9. The original price of a jacket is $36.95. The jacket is discounted by 25%. Before tax, which of the following best represents the cost of the jacket?
    a. $27.34
    b. $27.71
    c. $28.11
    d. $28.82
    e. $29.56

10. The number 123 is the 11th term in a sequence with a constant rate of change. Which of the following sequences has this number as its 11th term?
    a. 5, 17, 29, 41, ...
    b. 3, 15, 27, 39, ...
    c. −1, 11, 23, 35, ...
    d. 1, 13, 25, 37, ...
    e. 3, 17, 23, 40, ...

11. What is the product of four squared and six?
    a. 22
    b. 28
    c. 55
    d. 96
    e. 104

12. A rectangular prism has a length of 14.3 cm, a width of 8.9 cm, and a height of 11.7 cm. Which of the following is the best estimate for the volume of the rectangular prism?
  a. 1,287 cm$^3$
  b. 1,386 cm$^3$
  c. 1,512 cm$^3$
  d. 1,573 cm$^3$
  e. 1,620 cm$^3$

13. Each month, Aisha invests twice the amount invested the previous month. If she invested $26.25 during the first month, how much did she invest during the sixth month?
  a. $157.50
  b. $420.00
  c. $768.50
  d. $840.00
  e. $900.00

14. Find the value of $x$ in the figure below:

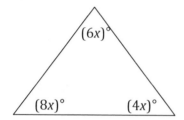

  a. 10
  b. 16
  c. 18
  d. 40
  e. 60

15. Elijah drove 45 miles to his job in an hour and ten minutes in the morning. On the way home in the evening, however, traffic was much heavier and the same trip took an hour and a half. What was his average speed in miles per hour for the round trip?
  a. 30
  b. $32\frac{1}{2}$
  c. $33\frac{3}{4}$
  d. 40
  e. 45

16. Chan receives a bonus from his job. He pays 30% in taxes, gives 30% to charity, and uses another 25% to pay off an old debt. He has $600 left. What was the total amount of Chan's bonus?
   a. $3000
   b. $3200
   c. $3600
   d. $4000
   e. $4200

17. If $3x + 5 = 11$, then $x$ = ?
   a. 1
   b. 2
   c. 3
   d. 4
   e. 6

18. Which of the following fractions is halfway between 2/5 and 4/9?
   a. 2/3
   b. 2/20
   c. 17/40
   d. 19/45
   e. 7/10

19. Solve for $y$ in the following equation if $x$ = -3
       $y = x + 5$
   a. y = -2
   b. y = 2
   c. y = 3
   d. y = 6
   e. y = 8

20. Which of the following is the symbol that represents the negative square root of 100?
   a. $\sqrt{-100}$
   b. $\sqrt{100}$
   c. $\sqrt{10}$
   d. $-\sqrt{10}$
   e. $-\sqrt{100}$

21. Anna wants to buy a new bicycle that costs $125, but she currently only has $40. If Anna can earn $5 each week for doing chores around the house, how many weeks will it take for Anna have enough money to buy the bicycle?
   a. 3 weeks
   b. 8 weeks
   c. 17 weeks
   d. 20 weeks
   e. 25 weeks

22. A sequence is formed from the equation, $y = 6x + 2$, where $x$ represents the term number and $y$ represents the value of the term. What is the value of the 18th term in the sequence?

 a. 98
 b. 104
 c. 110
 d. 116
 e. 120

23. Simplify $\frac{5}{9} \times \frac{3}{4}$.

 a. $\frac{5}{12}$

 b. $\frac{8}{13}$

 c. $\frac{20}{27}$

 d. $\frac{47}{36}$

 e. $\frac{52}{26}$

24. Rachel spent $24.15 on vegetables. She bought 2 pounds of onions, 3 pounds of carrots, and $1\frac{1}{2}$ pounds of mushrooms. If the onions cost $3.69 per pound, and the carrots cost $4.29 per pound, what is the price per pound of mushrooms?

 a. $2.25
 b. $2.35
 c. $2.60
 d. $2.80
 e. $3.10

25. At a picnic, cans of soda are put into a cooler. In the cooler, there are 12 colas, 6 diet colas, 9 lemon-limes, 2 root beers, 4 ginger ales, and 3 orange sodas. What would be the probability of reaching into the cooler without looking and pulling out a ginger ale?

 a. $\frac{1}{9}$

 b. $\frac{1}{8}$

 c. $\frac{1}{6}$

 d. $\frac{1}{5}$

 e. $\frac{1}{3}$

# Answers and Explanations

## Section 1: Quantitative

1. B: Translate this word problem into a mathematical equation. Let the number of Janice's phone calls = $x$. Let the number of Elaina's phone calls = $x + 23$. Let the number June's phone calls = $x + 14$. Add their calls together and subtract 25 calls:
$= x + x + 23 + x + 14 - 25$
$= 3x + 37 - 25$
$= 3x + 12$.

2. C: To answer this question, notice that this figure is a regular hexagon, having 6 equal sides and angles. The part painted darker can be represented by $\frac{1}{6}$. The part painted lighter is clearly $\frac{1}{2}$, which is equivalent to $\frac{3}{6}$. The whole figure is represented by the number 1. So, 1 minus $\frac{1}{6}$ minus $\frac{3}{6}$ equals $\frac{2}{6}$ which is equivalent to $\frac{1}{3}$. Therefore, the equation, $1 - \frac{1}{6} - \frac{1}{2} = \frac{1}{3}$ best models the part of the figure Olga left white.

3. A: Since there are 100 cm in a meter, on a 1:100 scale drawing, each centimeter represents one meter. Therefore, an area of one square centimeter on the drawing represents one square meter in actuality. Since the area of the room in the scale drawing is 30 cm$^2$, the room's actual area is 30 m$^2$.

Another way to determine the area of the room is to write and solve an equation, such as this one:
$\frac{l}{100} \cdot \frac{w}{100} = 30$ cm$^2$ , where $l$ and $w$ are the dimensions of the actual room

$$\frac{lw}{1000} = 30 \text{ cm}^2$$
$$lw = 300{,}000 \text{ cm}^2$$
$$\text{Area} = 300{,}000 \text{ cm}^2$$

Since this is not one of the answer choices, convert cm$^2$ to m$^2$: $300{,}000$ cm$^2 \cdot \frac{1 \text{ m}}{100 \text{ cm}} \cdot \frac{1 \text{ m}}{100 \text{ cm}} = 30$ m$^2$.

4. E: The total amount of the bill is: $\frac{4}{x} = \frac{8}{100}$; $400 = 8x$; $x = \$50$.

5. C: The line graph shows the largest number of flights made during a month as 79 with the smallest number of flights made during a month as 54. The range is equal to the difference between the largest number of flights and smallest number of flights, i.e., $79 - 54 = 25$. Therefore, the range is equal to 25.

6. E: Segment $AD = 48$. Because the length of $CD$ is 2 times the length of $AB$, let $AB = x$ and let $CD = 2x$. Since $AB = BC$, let $BC = x$ also. The total length of $AD = AB + BC + CD = x + x + 2x = 4x = 48$. Thus, $x = 12$ and $BC + CD = x + 2x = 3x = 3 \times 12 = 36$.

7. C: The stock first increased by 10%, that is, by $10 (10% of $100) to $110 per share. Then, the price decreased by $11 (10% of $110) so that the sale price was $110-$11 = $99 per share, and the sale price for 50 shares was 99 x $50 = $4950.

8. D: We know that the first lap takes 50 seconds, and the second one takes 20% more time to complete. This can be written as an equation: $T_2 = 1.2 \times T_1$. In the equation, $T_1$ is the time required for the first lap, and $T_2$ is the time required for the second lap. So, you can put in the known information and have: $1.2 \times 50 = 60$ seconds. For the third lap, you would start with the equation: $T_3 = 1.2 \times T_2$. When you put in the numbers, you have: $1.2 \times 60 = 72$ seconds. Now, you can add the times for the three laps: $50 + 60 + 72 = 182$.

9. C: Supplementary angles add to 180 degrees. Therefore, the other angle is equal to the difference between 180 degrees and 34 degrees: $180 - 34 = 146$. Thus, the other angle measures 146°.

10. A: The distance given from the top to the bottom of the tire through the center is the diameter. Finding the distance the bike traveled in one complete roll of the tire is the same as finding the circumference. Using the formula, $C = \pi d$, we multiply 27 by $\pi$. From the first mark to the fourth, the tire rolls three times. Then, you would multiply by 3, and the equation would be $3(27\pi)$.

11. E: First: Add the known values together: $5 + 10 + 12 + 13 = 40$. Now, set up an equation with the sum of the known values in the divisor. Then, put the number of values in the dividend.

For this question, you have 5 values. So, you would write the equation as $\frac{40+?}{5} = 9.6$. Now, multiply both sides by 5: $5 \times \frac{40+?}{5} = 9.6 \times 5$. You are left with $40+? = 48$. Now, subtract 40 from both sides: $40 - 40+? = 48 - 40$. Now, you know that the missing value is 8.

12. A: The events are independent since Sarah replaces the first die. The probability of two independent events can be found using the formula $P(A \text{ and } B) = P(A) \cdot P(B)$. The probability of pulling out a blue die is $\frac{2}{12}$. The probability of pulling out a green die is $\frac{4}{12}$. The probability of pulling out a blue die and a green die is $\frac{2}{12} \cdot \frac{4}{12}$, which simplifies to $\frac{1}{18}$.

13. D: Isolate $a$: $a = 8b + 6 + 16$. Thus, $a = 8b + 22$. Next add 3 to both side of the equation: $a + 3 = 8b + 22 + 3$
$= 8b + 25$.

14. A: The cost per ounce can be calculated by dividing the cost of the bag by the number of ounces the bag contains. Thus, the cost per ounce can be calculated by writing $9.85 ÷ 16, which equals approximately $0.62 per ounce.

Copyright © Mometrix Media. You have been licensed one copy of this document for personal use only. Any other reproduction or redistribution is strictly prohibited. All rights reserved.

15. B: The slope of a line describes the change in the dependent variable divided by the change in the independent variable, i.e. the change in y over the change in x. To calculate the slope, consider any two points on the line. Let the first point be (1, 14), and let the second point be (2, 28).

$$\frac{y_2 - y_1}{x_2 - x_1} = \frac{28 - 14}{2 - 1} = \frac{14}{1} = 14$$

16. B: Since 1 foot equals 0.3048 meters, the following proportion can be written: $\frac{1}{0.3048} = \frac{12}{x}$. Solving for $x$ gives $x = 3.6576$, which rounds to 3.66. Thus, the length of the bridge is approximately 3.66 meters.

17. C: There are 36 months in 3 years. The following proportion may be written: $\frac{450}{3} = \frac{x}{36}$. The equation $3x = 16200$, may be solved for $x$. Dividing both sides of the equation by 3 gives $x = 5,400$.

18. D: The area of the shaded region must be equal to the area of the square minus the areas of the two triangular areas ΔACD and ΔBEF. The area of a triangle is given by $A = \frac{1}{2}bh$, where $b$ is the base and $h$ is the height. Since ΔACD and ΔBEF are both right triangles, one of the orthogonal sides is the base and the other is the height. Further, since AE = EB and BF = FC, it follows that EB = BF = 5, this being one half the side AB. Thus, $A_{ADC} = \frac{1}{2}(10 \times 10) = 50$, and $A_{BEF} = \frac{1}{2}(5 \times 5) = 12.5$. The area of the square is the product of its two sides, or 10 × 10 = 100. Therefore, for the shaded region, A = 100 – 50 – 12.5 = 37.5.

19. C: Remember to use the order of operations when simplifying this equation. The acronym *PEMDAS* will help you remember the correct order: Parenthesis, Exponentiation, Multiplication/Division, Addition/Subtraction.
4(6 – 3)² – (-2)
First, simplify the parentheses: 4 x 3² – (-2)
Next, simplify the exponent: 4 x 9 – (-2)
Then multiply: 36 – (-2)
Finally, subtract: 36 – (-2) = 36 + 2 = 38

20. C: Isolate the variable on one side of the equal sign by adding 2 to both sides of the equation. This yields $\sqrt{x} = 8 + 2 = 10$. Now, solve the equation by squaring both sides: $x = 10^2 = 100$.

21. C: The original triangle was reflected across the x-axis. When reflecting across the x-axis, the x-values of each point remain the same, but the y-values of the points will be opposites.
$(1,4) \rightarrow (1,-4), (5,\ 4) \rightarrow (5,-4), (3,8) \rightarrow (3,-8)$.

22. B: To solve this problem, you need to find the time needed to drive 275 miles at a speed of 55 miles per hour. If $rate \times time = distance$, then $time = distance \div rate$:

$$r \times t = d$$

$$\frac{r \times t}{r} = \frac{d}{r}$$

$$t = \frac{d}{r}$$

$275 \div 55 = 5$ hours
The truck driver needs to arrive at 9:30 p.m., so subtract 5 hours from 9:30. The truck driver needs to leave at 4:30 p.m. to arrive on time.

23. E: Attendance in 2004 decreased from about 12,000 to 10,000 visitors. In 2005 it rebounded to 15,000 visitors, an increase of 5,000. This is the greatest year-to-year increase shown on the chart.

24. A: Add the coefficients of the 'x-terms' together as follows: 5x + 4x = 9x
Add the coefficients of the 'y-terms' as follows: –2y + y = –y
Put the x- and y-terms back into the same equation: 9x – y.

25. E: Out of the twelve numbers, half are even. That means there is a 50% chance that the spinner will land on an even number.

## Section 2: Reading Comprehension

1. D: Various parts of the article are intended to scare (choice A), warn (choice B), and inspire (choice C) people, but the primary purpose of the article is to offer practical advice about what products people should buy and how to use their available resources to make responsible decisions for the future of our planet.

2. A: The author begins the third paragraph with, "You can continue to make a difference for the planet in how you use what you bought and the resources you have available." This sentence makes the connection between the second paragraph which deals with what people should buy and the third paragraph which makes suggestions for how to use what they have.

3. B: The author does suggest that people should use less water and energy (choice A), but these are only two suggestions among many and not the main idea of the article. The article does not say that people are destroying the earth (choice C) or make a suggestion that people organize their acquaintances (choice D).

4. D: The author presents the problems of global warming and the rapid depletion of the planet's natural resources and offers several practical suggestions for how to stop global warming and use remaining resources judiciously.

5. E: The author makes suggestions to use less water (choice B) and buy locally grown food (choice D), but they are not suggested as the place to begin saving the planet. The author does not suggest getting rid of products that are not earth friendly (choice A). The author states: "Participation begins with our everyday choices."

6. C: The author does not mention running out of resources in a specific time period (choice A), the cost of water and energy (choice B), or the possibility of hardship for local farmers (choice D).

7. D: Paragraph 1 states that Aberystwyth is located on the West Coast of Wales.

8. C: The essay provides information on various aspects of the town of Aberystwyth, providing a portrait of the town as a whole.

9. A: Situated means to be located in a certain place.

10. B: In an essay that is factual, proclaiming that the scenery is "gorgeous" or that a town is a "hidden luxury" is an opinion.

11. B: Paragraph 3 states that two main languages are traditionally spoken in Aberystwyth.

12. C: Paragraph 1 states, "A market town refers to European areas that have the right to have markets, which differentiates it from a city or village."

13. D: Paragraph 2 states, "Constitution Hill is a hill on the north end of Aberystwyth, which provides excellent views of Cardigan Bay and which is supported by the Aberystwyth Electric Cliff Railway."

14. A: Paragraph 1 explains that Aberystwyth is best known as an education center, and this is repeated in paragraph 3, which states that Aberystwyth is best known for its educational services.

15. B: While some of the other choices are mentioned in the selection, they do not adequately explain what the entire selection is about.

16. A: From the first paragraph, you can determine that Gawaine has little or no interest in becoming a knight.

17. D: Gawaine is said to be tall and sturdy, but he would run away and hide at the smallest sign of trouble.

18. D: "His better nature" is one way of talking about a person's deeper character.

19. C: This forms part of the answer to the professor's question, "Are the dragons particularly bad this year?"

20. D: Choice A is not mentioned in the text, and the other choices do not directly answer the question.

21. C: The passage states that he was given this title since he was the first to explain how organisms change over time.

22. A: The tone and purpose of this passage is to inform the reader.

23. E: The passage explains that finches with longer, sharper beaks were able to reach insects more easily than finches with shorter beaks, giving them an advantage over the other finches on the island.

24. B: The island finches were different from the mainland finches, so their geographical separation over time increased the diversity of finches.

25. D: The passage states that the island finches differed from the mainland finches by the shape of their beaks and in their diet.

26. C: An archipelago is a large group or chain of islands.

27. D: The article deals primarily with the ways the colonists fed themselves: their crops and the foods they hunted. While it also describes New Zealand's prehistory, the main focus is on food sources.

28. D: The passage states that the first settlers were forced to rely on fishing for their food.

29. A: When an increased population had driven a major food source to extinction, they began to fight for control over the remaining food supply.

30. D: The article tells us that coconuts did not grow in New Zealand, and that some of the other crops would grow only on North Island.

- 117 -

31. A: The sweet potato provided a winter food source through storage, allowing the population to increase.

32. C: Both roads in the woods are more or less equally covered in leaves. One is only a little more traveled than the other, but this is enough for the narrator to choose the less-traveled path.

33. C: Looking back on the memory, the narrator is proud that he "chose the [road] less traveled by," and he will make sure that other people know that, too.

34. D: The poem is based on the narrator having to decide upon a path based only on his own personality and how well traveled the road is. It is a decision that he must make alone.

35. E: The narrator thinks that whatever road he chooses will say something about his character. He waits a long time because he wants to be sure of his choice.

36. B: The narrator wants to be as unique as he can, and so takes the road less traveled. However, he cannot be truly unique, as he is not the first person to have walked that road.

37. D: The main argument is stated in paragraph 4: "With the progression and extreme convenience of technology, printed books are going to soon become a thing of the past."

38. C: Paragraph 1 explains how stories have progressed, beginning with oral tradition and past the invention of the printing press. In context with the rest of the essay, this paragraph is important in explaining how stories progress and are provided within society.

39. A: In paragraph 1, it is stated that oral tradition was the main medium for storytelling before the invention of the printing press.

40. E: It is not a fact that "sliding a finger across the screen or pressing a button to move onto the next page is just as satisfying to the reader." Satisfaction is not something universal that can be proven for every reader. This statement is an opinion.

**Section 3: Verbal**

1. B: When someone is abroad, it usually means that they are away, overseas, or in a foreign country.

2. D: When someone ruminates, it means that they are reflecting, thinking, or brainstorming about something or someone.

3. A: When something is described as concise, it usually means that it is brief or compact.

4. A: When someone mourns, it means that they are crying or filled with regret.

5. A: Residence is a place where a person lives. So, a home is the best answer choice.

6. C: Levity means happiness or silliness.

7. B: When something is described as rash, it usually means that it is careless or bold.

8. C: When it is said that someone has been banished, it means that they have been removed or dismissed from a place.

9. B: When you are extended an opportunity, you are being offered a chance to try something.

10. E: To disable means that something is damaged or harmed.

11. D: An object that is fragile is something that can be broken very easily. So, one could say that the object is delicate.

12. D: A loyal person is someone who is committed and faithful.

13. D: The principle is something that is the standard or source. This should be confused with principal who may the head of a school or an organization.

14. C: To assess something is to evaluate or determine something.

15. C: If somebody is moral, it means that they are honest or good and correct in their behavior.

16. C: Something that is superior is understood to be preferable or better.

17. B: A remark is a statement or comment.

18. B: Specify is when you indicate or name something to give a clear understanding to others. For example, there are several trees in a yard, and you are talking about one tree. So, you would need to be clear or specify which tree that you meant.

19. A: To commence something is to begin or start something.

20. B: Something that is moving swiftly is something that is moving at a high speed or quickly.

21. A: Someone that is wily is clever or mischievous. For example, a child who avoids something that he or she doesn't want to do will be creative with excuses or deceptive about their plans.

22. C: Humane is another word for friendly. Saying someone is humane is the same as saying that they are very helpful and generous.

23. B: When someone is asserting something, they are insisting or arguing that something is the case.

24. E: A situation that is perilous is one that is risky or hazardous.

25. C: To donate means to offer a service or gift something as a contribution.

26. C: When something is finite, we mean that it is limited or fixed. Saying that there is a finite amount of gold in the world has the same meaning as saying that there is a limited amount of gold in the world.

27. B: When somebody is docile, it means that they are obedient or easily led. A student who respects and obeys their teachers will be a docile student.

28. C: To taint has a similar meaning to harm or damage. If you say that a shirt is tainted, for example, you are saying that the shirt is ruined or damaged.

29. D: When a person falters, we mean that they stumbled or hesitated. For example, a good character in a story has to make a difficult decision, and he or she struggles to make the decision in time. So, we could say that the character faltered to make a decision.

30. D: Something that is done suddenly means that it is done unexpectedly or without warning. For example, saying that the car stopped suddenly and saying it stopped unexpectedly convey the same meaning.

31. C: The analogy focuses on a characteristic of historians who need to consider an event with the surrounding context of time before and after an event. The best choice is the comparison to a native who has insight about his or her village or country and provide context to events of their area.

32. B: This analogy is about the use of geography and how one thing that it studies is mountains. Among the choices, one use of history is the study of events and how they have made an important influence.

33. E: This comparison is about the antonyms exhale and inhale. The other answer choices are synonyms, and choice E has the antonyms of consent and prohibit.

34. D: This comparison is about the synonyms of fiction and myth. The other answer choices are antonyms or something that is incompatible with nonfiction. So, the correct choice that remains is biography.

35. C: A simple sentence for this analogy could be "An astronomer's task is to encounter new things." The other users in the answer choices do not match with this sentence, and their "tasks" are not typical jobs for them. Answer choice C could be written as "A prophet's task is to inform about new things."

36. B: This analogy is about the homonyms *dual* and *duel* which sound similar but have different meanings. The only answer choice that makes sense is choice B which has the homonyms of *seam* and *seem*.

37. A: This analogy of degree focuses on a symptom that is part of an illness. The best answer is choice A which starts with a bacteria that develops into an infection.

38. A: Evidence that is used in a court of law can be condemning for someone by bringing a punishment on him or her. The best comparison for this question is choice A where the use of a generator is to restore energy or electricity to something.

39. C: *Liberty* and *freedom* are close synonyms, and *sincere* is a close synonym of *faithful*.

40. C: This comparison is about the antonyms *masculine* and *feminine*. The other answer choices are synonyms. So, the best answer is choice C which has the antonyms *community* and *individual*.

41. B: An artist brings imagination to complete their tasks and help others. In a similar way, an advisor uses clarity to complete their tasks and help others.

42. D: This comparison shows that one characteristic of a temple is that it is sacred. The best answer choice is the comparison of a sanctuary to its loftiness or grandness and beauty.

43. E: A gourmet is a person who is very familiar with food, and this person would fall under the category of a critic. With the topic of food in mind, a spice is an item that provides flavor to meals and can come under the category of ingredient.

44. C: As a part to whole analogy, a summit is the highest point of a mountain. Now, you need to judge how a king is a part of a whole. The best answer is choice C as a member of a monarchy government.

45. A: The analogy highlights a product to producer relationship. The tactics of a mission are made and developed by marines. In a similar way, data is developed by a researcher.

46. B: A chamber is needed to contain or hold items. Choice A is nearly a product to producer as some rulers on thrones can be intimidating to the point that people bow or cower before the throne. Choice C is a characteristic analogy. Answer choice D is a synonym. Answer choice E is a category analogy. So, the best choice is B as an agenda is used to organize the use of time.

47. D: This analogy is about the homonyms *altar* and *alter*. The correct answer choice D has the homonyms *rain* and *reign*.

48. B: To help more patients, a physician would study the nutritional value of certain items and harm from other items. So, this analogy focuses on a user. The other answer choices do not focus on the relationship of an item or field of study and a user, or they make incorrect connections. Thus, the best answer choice is choice B because wildlife would be studied by a guide for future tours.

49. B: The terms *bravery* and *cowardice* are antonyms in this analogy. So, the best answer choice is the one that is an antonym for *comedy*, and the best choice is choice B for *grief.*

50. E: When we say that a child is *naïve*, we are naming one of their characteristics. The correct answer choice is choice E which has *disciplined* as a characteristic of a *soldier.*

51. B: This analogy focuses on the homonyms of *colonel* and *kernel*. So, the correct answer choice is the homonyms *serial* and *cereal.*

52. D: You may recall from science classes that protons and electrons are parts of an atom. A proton has a positive charge, and an electron has a negative charge. So, the comparison focuses on these as opposites or antonyms. Therefore, the best answer choice is choice D which compares *potent* and *ineffective* as antonyms.

53. D: A documentary can be used by a protestor to bring more attention to his or her cause. So, this analogy highlights the comparison of someone who uses something. The best answer choice is choice D which has a *rotor* being used by a *mechanic.*

54. C: Again, we have a homonym analogy with the terms *tear* and *tier.* You are provided with the term *air*, and the best choice available is choice C which has *heir.*

55. B: An *epidemic* is a disease that is far reaching. The same definition applies to *plague*. So, you know that we are working with a comparison of synonyms. You are supplied with the term *vigor* which means high energy and strength. So, the best available synonym is *endurance.*

56. D: You may recognize that *eternal* means that something continues without an end. *Momentary* means that something is brief or short-lived. So, the best answer choice is choice D which has the antonyms of *exotic* (i.e., unusual or mysterious) and *ordinary* (i.e., plain or familiar).

57. A: Often, an open field of a meadow is described as a peaceful and restful place to rest. So, one could say that a meadow has the characteristic of being tranquil. The best match for this analogy would be choice A as a *tributary* (i.e., river or stream) can be a *consoling* or restful place to visit.

58. D: This analogy highlights another homonym relationship. The other answer choices are terms that rhyme or have no understandable relationship. So, the best answer choice is choice D of *carat* and *carrot.*

59. A: An *aviator* is a person who flies an aircraft. So, this relationship can be understood as an *aviator* is responsible for flying an aircraft to a certain *destination*. In a similar way, choice A can be understood as a *sculptor* or artist is responsible for creating *original* works of art.

60. E: A *constellation* is a group of stars that form an outline of a person, animal, or object. So, this analogy can be understood as a whole moving to a part. The *constellation* is the whole, and a *star* is a part of the whole. Now, the best answer choice would be choice E as an *orchestra* is a group of musicians playing music with their respective *instruments*. Thus, an *instrument* would a part of the whole *orchestra*.

## Section 4: Quantitative

1. B: The number of one-fourths contained in $8\frac{1}{2}$ can be determined by dividing $8\frac{1}{2}$ by $\frac{1}{4}$. In order to find the quotient, $8\frac{1}{2}$ can be multiplied by the reciprocal of $\frac{1}{4}$, or 4. Thus, the quotient can be found by writing $\frac{17}{2} \times 4$, which equals 34.

2. C: The equation that represents the relationship between the position number, $n$, and the value of the term, $a_n$, is $a_n = -3n + 8$. Notice each $n$ is multiplied by –3, with 8 added to that value. Substituting position number 1 for $n$ gives $a_n = -3(1) + 8$, which equals 5. Substitution of the remaining position numbers does not provide a counterexample to this procedure.

3. E: A triangle with an obtuse angle (an angle greater than 90°) is called an obtuse triangle.

4. D: Since the snow will fall at a constant rate, the snowfall follows a directly proportional relationship. Then, $Total\ Snowfall = (Snowfall\ rate) \times$ $(Number\ of\ hours\ of\ snowfall)$, $t = 2h$. In Answer A, the values were set up as an inversely proportional relationship. In Answer B, the snowfall rate was incorrectly added to the number of hours of snowfall. In Answer C, the snowfall rate was incorrectly subtracted from the number of hours of snowfall.

5. B: Whenever the data includes an extreme outlier, such as 39, the median is the best representation of the data. The mean would include that score and heavily skew the data.

6. B: Angles that form a straight line add up to 180 degrees. Such angles are sometimes referred to as being "supplementary."
60 + 2x = 180
2x = 120
x = 60

7. E: In this problem, if you do not know how to solve, try filling in the answer choices to see which one checks out. Many math problems may be solved by a guess and check method when you have a selection of answer choices.
27 – x = -5
x = 32

8. C: The order of operations states that numbers with exponents must be evaluated first. Thus, the expression can be rewritten as $64 + 12 \div 4 + 64 \times 3$. Next, multiplication and division must be computed as they appear from left to right in the expression. Thus, the expression can be further simplified as $64 + 3 + 192$, which equals 259.

9. B: The discounted price is 25% less than the original price. Therefore, the discounted price can be written as $36.95 - ((0.25)(36.95))$, which equals approximately 27.71. Thus, the discounted price of the jacket is $27.71.

10. B: All given sequences have a constant difference of 12. Subtraction of 12 from the starting term, given for Choice B, gives a $y$-intercept of –9. The equation $123 = 12x - 9$ can thus be written. Solving for $x$ gives $x = 11$; therefore, 123 is indeed the 11th term of this

sequence. Manual computation of the 11th term by adding the constant difference of 12 also reveals 123 as the value of the 11th term of this sequence.

11. D: Turn the word problem into an equation. Remember that product means multiplication: $4^2 \times 6 = 96$.

12. C: The dimensions of the rectangular prism can be rounded to 14 cm, 9 cm, and 12 cm. The volume of a rectangular prism can be determined by finding the product of the length, width, and height. Therefore, the volume is approximately equal to $14 \times 9 \times 12$, or 1,512 $cm^3$.

13. D: The amount Aisha invests doubles each month. Thus, the invested amounts for months 1 – 6 are as follows: $26.25, $52.50, $105, $210, $420, and $840. She invests $840 during the sixth month.

14. A: The sum of the measures of the angles in a triangle equals 180°. Use the numbers given in the figure to make the following equation:
$6x + 8x + 4x = 180$
$18x = 180$
$x = 10$

15. C: To determine this, first determine the total distance of the round trip. This is twice the 45 miles of the one-way trip to work in the morning, or 90 miles. Then, to determine the total amount of time Elijah spent on the round trip, first convert his travel times into minutes. One hour and ten minutes equals 70 minutes, and an hour and a half equals 90 minutes. So, Elijah's total travel time was 70 + 90 = 160 minutes. Elijah's average speed can now be determined in miles per minute:
$$Speed = \frac{90miles}{160min} = 0.5625 \text{ miles per minute}$$
Finally, to convert this average speed to miles per hour, multiply by 60, since there are 60 minutes in an hour:
$$\text{Average speed (mph)} = 60 \times 0.5625 = 33.75 \text{ miles per hour}$$

16. D: Besides the $600 he has remaining; Chan has paid out a total of 85% (30% + 30% +25%) of his bonus for the expenses described in the question. Therefore, the $600 represents the remaining 15%. Remember that 15% can be written as 15/100. To determine his total bonus, solve $\frac{15}{100}x = 600$. So, $x = \frac{100}{15} \times 600 = 4,000$ dollars.

17. B: Since 11 – 5 = 6, then $3x = 6$, and $x = \frac{6}{3} = 2$.

18. D: Find the common denominator for the two fractions so that you can compare them. You can use the common denominator of 45, as follows:
2/5 = 18/45
4/9 = 20/45
Look at the numerators: 18 and 20. The number halfway between them is 19, so the answer is 19/45

19. B: $y = x + 5$, and you were told that $x = -3$. Fill in the missing information for $x$, then solve.
$y = (-3) + 5$
$y = 2$

20. E: You would write the negative square root of 100 as follows: $-\sqrt{100}$

21. C: The equation to determine how Anna can earn the $125 is set up as: $Weekly\ Pay \times Number\ of\ Weeks + Money\ Anna\ Already\ Has = \$125$. If $w$ = number of weeks, substitute for the remaining values to get the equation: $\$5w + \$40 = \$125$. To solve that equation, start by subtracting $40 from both sides: $\$5w = \$85$. Then, divide both sides by 5 to get $h = 17$.

22. C: The value of the 18ᵗʰ term can be found by substituting 18 for the variable, $x$, in the equation, $y = 6x + 2$. Doing so gives: $y = 6(18) + 2$, or $y = 110$. Therefore, the value of the 18ᵗʰ term is 110.

23. A: When multiplying fractions, multiply the terms straight across the fraction: $\frac{5}{9} \times \frac{3}{4} = \frac{15}{36}$. Then, simplify the fraction. Since 15 and 36 are both multiples of 3, divide each term by 3 to reach the final result: $\frac{5}{12}$.

24. C: To answer this question, we first determine the total cost of the onions and carrots, since these prices are given. This will equal (2 x $3.69 + 3 x $4.29) = $20.25. Next, this sum is subtracted from the total cost of the vegetables to determine the cost of the mushrooms: $24.15 - $20.25 = $3.90. Finally, the cost of the mushrooms is divided by the quantity in lbs to determine the cost per lb:

Cost per lb $= \dfrac{\$3.90}{1.5} = \$2.60$

25. A: There are 36 total cans in the cooler. Four of the cans are Ginger Ale. Therefore, there is a $\frac{4}{36} = \frac{1}{9}$ probability of pulling a Ginger Ale out of the cooler.

# Secret Key #1 - Time is Your Greatest Enemy

## *Pace Yourself*

Wear a watch. At the beginning of the test, check the time (or start a chronometer on your watch to count the minutes), and check the time after every few questions to make sure you are "on schedule."

If you are forced to speed up, do it efficiently. Usually one or more answer choices can be eliminated without too much difficulty. Above all, don't panic. Don't speed up and just begin guessing at random choices. By pacing yourself, and continually monitoring your progress against your watch, you will always know exactly how far ahead or behind you are with your available time. If you find that you are one minute behind on the test, don't skip one question without spending any time on it, just to catch back up. Take 15 fewer seconds on the next four questions, and after four questions you'll have caught back up. Once you catch back up, you can continue working each problem at your normal pace.

Furthermore, don't dwell on the problems that you were rushed on. If a problem was taking up too much time and you made a hurried guess, it must be difficult. The difficult questions are the ones you are most likely to miss anyway, so it isn't a big loss. It is better to end with more time than you need than to run out of time.

Lastly, sometimes it is beneficial to slow down if you are constantly getting ahead of time. You are always more likely to catch a careless mistake by working more slowly than quickly, and among very high-scoring test takers (those who are likely to have lots of time left over), careless errors affect the score more than mastery of material.

# Secret Key #2 - Guessing is not Guesswork

You probably know that guessing is a good idea. Unlike other standardized tests, there is no penalty for getting a wrong answer. Even if you have no idea about a question, you still have a 20-25% chance of getting it right.

Most test takers do not understand the impact that proper guessing can have on their score. Unless you score extremely high, guessing will significantly contribute to your final score.

## Monkeys Take the Test

What most test takers don't realize is that to insure that 20-25% chance, you have to guess randomly. If you put 20 monkeys in a room to take this test, assuming they answered once per question and behaved themselves, on average they would get 20-25% of the questions correct. Put 20 test takers in the room, and the average will be much lower among guessed questions. Why?

1. The test writers intentionally write deceptive answer choices that "look" right. A test taker has no idea about a question, so he picks the "best looking" answer, which is often wrong. The monkey has no idea what looks good and what doesn't, so it will consistently be right about 20-25% of the time.
2. Test takers will eliminate answer choices from the guessing pool based on a hunch or intuition. Simple but correct answers often get excluded, leaving a 0% chance of being correct. The monkey has no clue, and often gets lucky with the best choice.

This is why the process of elimination endorsed by most test courses is flawed and detrimental to your performance. Test takers don't guess; they make an ignorant stab in the dark that is usually worse than random.

# $5 Challenge

Let me introduce one of the most valuable ideas of this course—the $5 challenge:

*You only mark your "best guess" if you are willing to bet $5 on it.*
*You only eliminate choices from guessing if you are willing to bet $5 on it.*

Why $5?  Five dollars is an amount of money that is small yet not insignificant, and can really add up fast (20 questions could cost you $100).  Likewise, each answer choice on one question of the test will have a small impact on your overall score, but it can really add up to a lot of points in the end.

The process of elimination IS valuable.  The following shows your chance of guessing it right:

| If you eliminate wrong answer choices until only this many remain: | Chance of getting it correct: |
|---|---|
| 1 | 100% |
| 2 | 50% |
| 3 | 33% |

However, if you accidentally eliminate the right answer or go on a hunch for an incorrect answer, your chances drop dramatically—to 0%.  By guessing among all the answer choices, you are GUARANTEED to have a shot at the right answer.

That's why the $5 test is so valuable.  If you give up the advantage and safety of a pure guess, it had better be worth the risk.

What we still haven't covered is how to be sure that whatever guess you make is truly random.  Here's the easiest way:

*Always pick the first answer choice among those remaining.*

Such a technique means that you have decided, **before you see a single test question**, exactly how you are going to guess, and since the order of choices tells you nothing about which one is correct, this guessing technique is perfectly random.

This section is not meant to scare you away from making educated guesses or eliminating choices; you just need to define when a choice is worth eliminating.  The $5 test, along with a pre-defined random guessing strategy, is the best way to make sure you reap all of the benefits of guessing.

# Secret Key #3 - Practice Smarter, Not Harder

Many test takers delay the test preparation process because they dread the awful amounts of practice time they think necessary to succeed on the test. We have refined an effective method that will take you only a fraction of the time.

There are a number of "obstacles" in the path to success. Among these are answering questions, finishing in time, and mastering test-taking strategies. All must be executed on the day of the test at peak performance, or your score will suffer. The test is a mental marathon that has a large impact on your future.

Just like a marathon runner, it is important to work your way up to the full challenge. So first you just worry about questions, and then time, and finally strategy:

## Success Strategy

1. Find a good source for practice tests.
2. If you are willing to make a larger time investment, consider using more than one study guide. Often the different approaches of multiple authors will help you "get" difficult concepts.
3. Take a practice test with no time constraints, with all study helps, "open book." Take your time with questions and focus on applying strategies.
4. Take a practice test with time constraints, with all guides, "open book."
5. Take a final practice test without open material and with time limits.

If you have time to take more practice tests, just repeat step 5. By gradually exposing yourself to the full rigors of the test environment, you will condition your mind to the stress of test day and maximize your success.

# Secret Key #4 - **Prepare, Don't Procrastinate**

Let me state an obvious fact: if you take the test three times, you will probably get three different scores. This is due to the way you feel on test day, the level of preparedness you have, and the version of the test you see. Despite the test writers' claims to the contrary, some versions of the test WILL be easier for you than others.

Since your future depends so much on your score, you should maximize your chances of success. In order to maximize the likelihood of success, you've got to prepare in advance. This means taking practice tests and spending time learning the information and test taking strategies you will need to succeed.

Never go take the actual test as a "practice" test, expecting that you can just take it again if you need to. Take all the practice tests you can on your own, but when you go to take the official test, be prepared, be focused, and do your best the first time!

# Secret Key #5 - Test Yourself

Everyone knows that time is money. There is no need to spend too much of your time or too little of your time preparing for the test. You should only spend as much of your precious time preparing as is necessary for you to get the score you need.

Once you have taken a practice test under real conditions of time constraints, then you will know if you are ready for the test or not.

If you have scored extremely high the first time that you take the practice test, then there is not much point in spending countless hours studying. You are already there.

Benchmark your abilities by retaking practice tests and seeing how much you have improved. Once you consistently score high enough to guarantee success, then you are ready.

If you have scored well below where you need, then knuckle down and begin studying in earnest. Check your improvement regularly through the use of practice tests under real conditions. Above all, don't worry, panic, or give up. The key is perseverance!

Then, when you go to take the test, remain confident and remember how well you did on the practice tests. If you can score high enough on a practice test, then you can do the same on the real thing.

# General Strategies

The most important thing you can do is to ignore your fears and jump into the test immediately. Do not be overwhelmed by any strange-sounding terms. You have to jump into the test like jumping into a pool—all at once is the easiest way.

## Make Predictions

As you read and understand the question, try to guess what the answer will be. Remember that several of the answer choices are wrong, and once you begin reading them, your mind will immediately become cluttered with answer choices designed to throw you off. Your mind is typically the most focused immediately after you have read the question and digested its contents. If you can, try to predict what the correct answer will be. You may be surprised at what you can predict.

Quickly scan the choices and see if your prediction is in the listed answer choices. If it is, then you can be quite confident that you have the right answer. It still won't hurt to check the other answer choices, but most of the time, you've got it!

## Answer the Question

It may seem obvious to only pick answer choices that answer the question, but the test writers can create some excellent answer choices that are wrong. Don't pick an answer just because it sounds right, or you believe it to be true. It MUST answer the question. Once you've made your selection, always go back and check it against the question and make sure that you didn't misread the question and that the answer choice does answer the question posed.

## Benchmark

After you read the first answer choice, decide if you think it sounds correct or not. If it doesn't, move on to the next answer choice. If it does, mentally mark that answer choice. This doesn't mean that you've definitely selected it as your answer choice, it just means that it's the best you've seen thus far. Go ahead and read the next choice. If the next choice is worse than the one you've already selected, keep going to the next answer choice. If the next choice is better than the choice you've already selected, mentally mark the new answer choice as your best guess.

The first answer choice that you select becomes your standard. Every other answer choice must be benchmarked against that standard. That choice is correct until proven otherwise by another answer choice beating it out. Once you've decided that no other answer choice seems as good, do one final check to ensure that your answer choice answers the question posed.

## Valid Information

Don't discount any of the information provided in the question. Every piece of information may be necessary to determine the correct answer. None of the information in the question is there to throw you off (while the answer choices will certainly have information to throw you off). If two seemingly unrelated topics are discussed, don't ignore either. You can be confident there is a relationship, or it wouldn't be included in the question, and you are probably going to have to determine what is that relationship to find the answer.

## Avoid "Fact Traps"

Don't get distracted by a choice that is factually true. Your search is for the answer that answers the question. Stay focused and don't fall for an answer that is true but irrelevant. Always go back to the question and make sure you're choosing an answer that actually answers the question and is not just a true statement. An answer can be factually correct, but it MUST answer the question asked. Additionally, two answers can both be seemingly correct, so be sure to read all of the answer choices, and make sure that you get the one that BEST answers the question.

## Milk the Question

Some of the questions may throw you completely off. They might deal with a subject you have not been exposed to, or one that you haven't reviewed in years. While your lack of knowledge about the subject will be a hindrance, the question itself can give you many clues that will help you find the correct answer. Read the question carefully and look for clues. Watch particularly for adjectives and nouns describing difficult terms or words that you don't recognize. Regardless of whether you completely understand a word or not, replacing it with a synonym, either provided or one you more familiar with, may help you to understand what the questions are asking. Rather than wracking your mind about specific detailed information concerning a difficult term or word, try to use mental substitutes that are easier to understand.

## The Trap of Familiarity

Don't just choose a word because you recognize it. On difficult questions, you may not recognize a number of words in the answer choices. The test writers don't put "make-believe" words on the test, so don't think that just because you only recognize all the words in one answer choice that that answer choice must be correct. If you only recognize words in one answer choice, then focus on that one. Is it correct? Try your best to determine if it is correct. If it is, that's great. If not, eliminate it. Each word and answer choice you eliminate increases your chances of getting the question correct, even if you then have to guess among the unfamiliar choices.

## Eliminate Answers

Eliminate choices as soon as you realize they are wrong. But be careful! Make sure you consider all of the possible answer choices. Just because one appears right, doesn't mean that the next one won't be even better! The test writers will usually put more than one good answer choice for every question, so read all of them. Don't worry if you are stuck between two that seem right.

By getting down to just two remaining possible choices, your odds are now 50/50. Rather than wasting too much time, play the odds. You are guessing, but guessing wisely because you've been able to knock out some of the answer choices that you know are wrong. If you are eliminating choices and realize that the last answer choice you are left with is also obviously wrong, don't panic. Start over and consider each choice again. There may easily be something that you missed the first time and will realize on the second pass.

## Tough Questions

If you are stumped on a problem or it appears too hard or too difficult, don't waste time. Move on! Remember though, if you can quickly check for obviously incorrect answer choices, your chances of guessing correctly are greatly improved. Before you completely give up, at least try to knock out a couple of possible answers. Eliminate what you can and then guess at the remaining answer choices before moving on.

## Brainstorm

If you get stuck on a difficult question, spend a few seconds quickly brainstorming. Run through the complete list of possible answer choices. Look at each choice and ask yourself, "Could this answer the question satisfactorily?" Go through each answer choice and consider it independently of the others. By systematically going through all possibilities, you may find something that you would otherwise overlook. Remember though that when you get stuck, it's important to try to keep moving.

## Read Carefully

Understand the problem. Read the question and answer choices carefully. Don't miss the question because you misread the terms. You have plenty of time to read each question thoroughly and make sure you understand what is being asked. Yet a happy medium must be attained, so don't waste too much time. You must read carefully, but efficiently.

## Face Value

When in doubt, use common sense. Always accept the situation in the problem at face value. Don't read too much into it. These problems will not require you to make huge leaps of logic. The test writers aren't trying to throw you off with a cheap trick. If you have to go beyond creativity and make a leap of logic in order to have an answer choice answer the question, then you should look at the other answer choices. Don't overcomplicate the problem by creating theoretical relationships or explanations that will warp time or space. These are normal problems rooted in reality. It's just that the applicable relationship or explanation may not be readily apparent and you have to figure things out. Use your common sense to interpret anything that isn't clear.

## Prefixes

If you're having trouble with a word in the question or answer choices, try dissecting it. Take advantage of every clue that the word might include. Prefixes and suffixes can be a huge help. Usually they allow you to determine a basic meaning. Pre- means before, post-means after, pro - is positive, de- is negative. From these prefixes and suffixes, you can get an idea of the general meaning of the word and try to put it into context. Beware though of any traps. Just because con- is the opposite of pro-, doesn't necessarily mean congress is the opposite of progress!

## Hedge Phrases

Watch out for critical hedge phrases, led off with words such as "likely," "may," "can," "sometimes," "often," "almost," "mostly," "usually," "generally," "rarely," and "sometimes." Question writers insert these hedge phrases to cover every possibility. Often an answer choice will be wrong simply because it leaves no room for exception. Unless the situation calls for them, avoid answer choices that have definitive words like "exactly," and "always."

## Switchback Words

Stay alert for "switchbacks." These are the words and phrases frequently used to alert you to shifts in thought. The most common switchback word is "but." Others include "although," "however," "nevertheless," "on the other hand," "even though," "while," "in spite of," "despite," and "regardless of."

## New Information

Correct answer choices will rarely have completely new information included. Answer choices typically are straightforward reflections of the material asked about and will directly relate to the question. If a new piece of information is included in an answer choice that doesn't even seem to relate to the topic being asked about, then that answer choice is likely incorrect. All of the information needed to answer the question is usually provided for you in the question. You should not have to make guesses that are unsupported or choose answer choices that require unknown information that cannot be reasoned from what is given.

## Time Management

On technical questions, don't get lost on the technical terms. Don't spend too much time on any one question. If you don't know what a term means, then odds are you aren't going to get much further since you don't have a dictionary. You should be able to immediately recognize whether or not you know a term. If you don't, work with the other clues that you have—the other answer choices and terms provided—but don't waste too much time trying to figure out a difficult term that you don't know.

## Contextual Clues

Look for contextual clues. An answer can be right but not the correct answer. The contextual clues will help you find the answer that is most right and is correct. Understand the context in which a phrase or statement is made. This will help you make important distinctions.

## Don't Panic

Panicking will not answer any questions for you; therefore, it isn't helpful. When you first see the question, if your mind goes blank, take a deep breath. Force yourself to mechanically go through the steps of solving the problem using the strategies you've learned.

## Pace Yourself

Don't get clock fever. It's easy to be overwhelmed when you're looking at a page full of questions, your mind is full of random thoughts and feeling confused, and the clock is ticking down faster than you would like. Calm down and maintain the pace that you have set for yourself. As long as you are on track by monitoring your pace, you are guaranteed to have enough time for yourself. When you get to the last few minutes of the test, it may seem like you won't have enough time left, but if you only have as many questions as you should have left at that point, then you're right on track!

## Answer Selection

The best way to pick an answer choice is to eliminate all of those that are wrong, until only one is left and confirm that is the correct answer. Sometimes though, an answer choice may immediately look right. Be careful! Take a second to make sure that the other choices are not equally obvious. Don't make a hasty mistake. There are only two times that you should stop before checking other answers. First is when you are positive that the answer choice you have selected is correct. Second is when time is almost out and you have to make a quick guess!

## Check Your Work

Since you will probably not know every term listed and the answer to every question, it is important that you get credit for the ones that you do know. Don't miss any questions through careless mistakes. If at all possible, try to take a second to look back over your answer selection and make sure you've selected the correct answer choice and haven't made a costly careless mistake (such as marking an answer choice that you didn't mean to mark). The time it takes for this quick double check should more than pay for itself in caught mistakes.

## Beware of Directly Quoted Answers

Sometimes an answer choice will repeat word for word a portion of the question or reference section. However, beware of such exact duplication. It may be a trap! More than likely, the correct choice will paraphrase or summarize a point, rather than being exactly the same wording.

## Slang

Scientific sounding answers are better than slang ones. An answer choice that begins "To compare the outcomes..." is much more likely to be correct than one that begins "Because some people insisted..."

## Extreme Statements

Avoid wild answers that throw out highly controversial ideas that are proclaimed as established fact. An answer choice that states the "process should be used in certain situations, if…" is much more likely to be correct than one that states the "process should be discontinued completely." The first is a calm rational statement and doesn't even make a definitive, uncompromising stance, using a hedge word "if" to provide wiggle room, whereas the second choice is a radical idea and far more extreme.

## Answer Choice Families

When you have two or more answer choices that are direct opposites or parallels, one of them is usually the correct answer. For instance, if one answer choice states "x increases" and another answer choice states "x decreases" or "y increases," then those two or three answer choices are very similar in construction and fall into the same family of answer choices. A family of answer choices consists of two or three answer choices, very similar in construction, but often with directly opposite meanings. Usually the correct answer choice will be in that family of answer choices. The "odd man out" or answer choice that doesn't seem to fit the parallel construction of the other answer choices is more likely to be incorrect.

# Special Report: How to Overcome Test Anxiety

The very nature of tests caters to some level of anxiety, nervousness, or tension, just as we feel for any important event that occurs in our lives. A little bit of anxiety or nervousness can be a good thing. It helps us with motivation, and makes achievement just that much sweeter. However, too much anxiety can be a problem, especially if it hinders our ability to function and perform.

"Test anxiety," is the term that refers to the emotional reactions that some test-takers experience when faced with a test or exam. Having a fear of testing and exams is based upon a rational fear, since the test-taker's performance can shape the course of an academic career. Nevertheless, experiencing excessive fear of examinations will only interfere with the test-taker's ability to perform and chance to be successful.

There are a large variety of causes that can contribute to the development and sensation of test anxiety. These include, but are not limited to, lack of preparation and worrying about issues surrounding the test.

## *Lack of Preparation*

Lack of preparation can be identified by the following behaviors or situations:

- Not scheduling enough time to study, and therefore cramming the night before the test or exam
- Managing time poorly, to create the sensation that there is not enough time to do everything
- Failing to organize the text information in advance, so that the study material consists of the entire text and not simply the pertinent information
- Poor overall studying habits

Worrying, on the other hand, can be related to both the test taker, or many other factors around him/her that will be affected by the results of the test. These include worrying about:

- Previous performances on similar exams, or exams in general
- How friends and other students are achieving
- The negative consequences that will result from a poor grade or failure

There are three primary elements to test anxiety. Physical components, which involve the same typical bodily reactions as those to acute anxiety (to be discussed below). Emotional factors have to do with fear or panic. Mental or cognitive issues concerning attention spans and memory abilities.

## Physical Signals

There are many different symptoms of test anxiety, and these are not limited to mental and emotional strain. Frequently there are a range of physical signals that will let a test taker know that he/she is suffering from test anxiety. These bodily changes can include the following:

- Perspiring
- Sweaty palms
- Wet, trembling hands
- Nausea
- Dry mouth
- A knot in the stomach
- Headache
- Faintness
- Muscle tension
- Aching shoulders, back and neck
- Rapid heart beat
- Feeling too hot/cold

To recognize the sensation of test anxiety, a test-taker should monitor him/herself for the following sensations:

- The physical distress symptoms as listed above
- Emotional sensitivity, expressing emotional feelings such as the need to cry or laugh too much, or a sensation of anger or helplessness
- A decreased ability to think, causing the test-taker to blank out or have racing thoughts that are hard to organize or control.

Though most students will feel some level of anxiety when faced with a test or exam, the majority can cope with that anxiety and maintain it at a manageable level. However, those who cannot are faced with a very real and very serious condition, which can and should be controlled for the immeasurable benefit of this sufferer. Naturally, these sensations lead to negative results for the testing experience. The most common effects of test anxiety have to do with nervousness and mental blocking.

## Nervousness

Nervousness can appear in several different levels:

- The test-taker's difficulty, or even inability to read and understand the questions on the test
- The difficulty or inability to organize thoughts to a coherent form
- The difficulty or inability to recall key words and concepts relating to the testing questions (especially essays)
- The receipt of poor grades on a test, though the test material was well known by the test taker

Conversely, a person may also experience mental blocking, which involves:

- Blanking out on test questions
- Only remembering the correct answers to the questions when the test has already finished.

Fortunately for test anxiety sufferers, beating these feelings, to a large degree, has to do with proper preparation. When a test taker has a feeling of preparedness, then anxiety will be dramatically lessened.

The first step to resolving anxiety issues is to distinguish which of the two types of anxiety are being suffered. If the anxiety is a direct result of a lack of preparation, this should be considered a normal reaction, and the anxiety level (as opposed to the test results) shouldn't be anything to worry about. However, if, when adequately prepared, the test-taker still panics, blanks out, or seems to overreact, this is not a fully rational reaction. While this can be considered normal too, there are many ways to combat and overcome these effects.

Remember that anxiety cannot be entirely eliminated, however, there are ways to minimize it, to make the anxiety easier to manage. Preparation is one of the best ways to minimize test anxiety. Therefore the following techniques are wise in order to best fight off any anxiety that may want to build.

To begin with, try to avoid cramming before a test, whenever it is possible. By trying to memorize an entire term's worth of information in one day, you'll be shocking your system, and not giving yourself a very good chance to absorb the information. This is an easy path to anxiety, so for those who suffer from test anxiety, cramming should not even be considered an option.

Instead of cramming, work throughout the semester to combine all of the material which is presented throughout the semester, and work on it gradually as the course goes by, making sure to master the main concepts first, leaving minor details for a week or so before the test.

To study for the upcoming exam, be sure to pose questions that may be on the examination, to gauge the ability to answer them by integrating the ideas from your texts, notes and lectures, as well as any supplementary readings.

If it is truly impossible to cover all of the information that was covered in that particular term, concentrate on the most important portions, that can be covered very well. Learn these concepts as best as possible, so that when the test comes, a goal can be made to use these concepts as presentations of your knowledge.

In addition to study habits, changes in attitude are critical to beating a struggle with test anxiety. In fact, an improvement of the perspective over the entire test-taking experience can actually help a test taker to enjoy studying and therefore improve the overall experience. Be certain not to overemphasize the significance of the grade - know that the result of the test is neither a reflection of self worth, nor is it a measure of intelligence; one grade will not predict a person's future success.

To improve an overall testing outlook, the following steps should be tried:
- Keeping in mind that the most reasonable expectation for taking a test is to expect to try to demonstrate as much of what you know as you possibly can.
- Reminding ourselves that a test is only one test; this is not the only one, and there will be others.
- The thought of thinking of oneself in an irrational, all-or-nothing term should be avoided at all costs.
- A reward should be designated for after the test, so there's something to look forward to. Whether it be going to a movie, going out to eat, or simply visiting friends, schedule it in advance, and do it no matter what result is expected on the exam.

Test-takers should also keep in mind that the basics are some of the most important things, even beyond anti-anxiety techniques and studying. Never neglect the basic social, emotional and biological needs, in order to try to absorb information. In order to best achieve, these three factors must be held as just as important as the studying itself.

## *Study Steps*

Remember the following important steps for studying:

- Maintain healthy nutrition and exercise habits. Continue both your recreational activities and social pass times. These both contribute to your physical and emotional well being.
- Be certain to get a good amount of sleep, especially the night before the test, because when you're overtired you are not able to perform to the best of your best ability.
- Keep the studying pace to a moderate level by taking breaks when they are needed, and varying the work whenever possible, to keep the mind fresh instead of getting bored.
- When enough studying has been done that all the material that can be learned has been learned, and the test taker is prepared for the test, stop studying and do something relaxing such as listening to music, watching a movie, or taking a warm bubble bath.

There are also many other techniques to minimize the uneasiness or apprehension that is experienced along with test anxiety before, during, or even after the examination. In fact, there are a great deal of things that can be done to stop anxiety from interfering with lifestyle and performance. Again, remember that anxiety will not be eliminated entirely, and it shouldn't be. Otherwise that "up" feeling for exams would not exist, and most of us depend on that sensation to perform better than usual. However, this anxiety has to be at a level that is manageable.

Of course, as we have just discussed, being prepared for the exam is half the battle right away. Attending all classes, finding out what knowledge will be expected on the exam, and knowing the exam schedules are easy steps to lowering anxiety. Keeping up with work will remove the need to cram, and efficient study habits will eliminate wasted time. Studying should be done in an ideal location for concentration, so that it is simple to become interested in the material and give it complete attention. A method such as SQ3R (Survey, Question, Read, Recite, Review) is a wonderful key to follow to make sure that the study habits are as effective as possible, especially in the case of learning from a textbook. Flashcards are great techniques for memorization. Learning to take good notes will mean that notes will be full of useful information, so that less sifting will need to be done to seek out what is pertinent for studying. Reviewing notes after class and then again on occasion will keep the information fresh in the mind. From notes that have been taken summary sheets and outlines can be made for simpler reviewing.

A study group can also be a very motivational and helpful place to study, as there will be a sharing of ideas, all of the minds can work together, to make sure that everyone understands, and the studying will be made more interesting because it will be a social occasion.

Basically, though, as long as the test-taker remains organized and self confident, with efficient study habits, less time will need to be spent studying, and higher grades will be achieved.

To become self confident, there are many useful steps. The first of these is "self talk." It has been shown through extensive research, that self-talk for students who suffer from test anxiety, should be well monitored, in order to make sure that it contributes to self confidence as opposed to sinking the student. Frequently the self talk of test-anxious students is negative or self-defeating, thinking that everyone else is smarter and faster, that they always mess up, and that if they don't do well, they'll fail the entire course. It is important to decreasing anxiety that awareness is made of self talk. Try writing any negative self thoughts and then disputing them with a positive statement instead. Begin self-encouragement as though it was a friend speaking. Repeat positive statements to help reprogram the mind to believing in successes instead of failures.

## Helpful Techniques

Other extremely helpful techniques include:

- Self-visualization of doing well and reaching goals
- While aiming for an "A" level of understanding, don't try to "overprotect" by setting your expectations lower. This will only convince the mind to stop studying in order to meet the lower expectations.
- Don't make comparisons with the results or habits of other students. These are individual factors, and different things work for different people, causing different results.
- Strive to become an expert in learning what works well, and what can be done in order to improve. Consider collecting this data in a journal.
- Create rewards for after studying instead of doing things before studying that will only turn into avoidance behaviors.
- Make a practice of relaxing - by using methods such as progressive relaxation, self-hypnosis, guided imagery, etc - in order to make relaxation an automatic sensation.
- Work on creating a state of relaxed concentration so that concentrating will take on the focus of the mind, so that none will be wasted on worrying.

- Take good care of the physical self by eating well and getting enough sleep.
- Plan in time for exercise and stick to this plan.

Beyond these techniques, there are other methods to be used before, during and after the test that will help the test-taker perform well in addition to overcoming anxiety.

Before the exam comes the academic preparation. This involves establishing a study schedule and beginning at least one week before the actual date of the test. By doing this, the anxiety of not having enough time to study for the test will be automatically eliminated. Moreover, this will make the studying a much more effective experience, ensuring that the learning will be an easier process. This relieves much undue pressure on the test-taker.

Summary sheets, note cards, and flash cards with the main concepts and examples of these main concepts should be prepared in advance of the actual studying time. A topic should never be eliminated from this process. By omitting a topic because it isn't expected to be on the test is only setting up the test-taker for anxiety should it actually appear on the exam. Utilize the course syllabus for laying out the topics that should be studied. Carefully go over the notes that were made in class, paying special attention to any of the issues that the professor took special care to emphasize while lecturing in class. In the textbooks, use the chapter review, or if possible, the chapter tests, to begin your review.

It may even be possible to ask the instructor what information will be covered on the exam, or what the format of the exam will be (for example, multiple choice, essay, free form, true-false). Additionally, see if it is possible to find out how many questions will be on the test. If a review sheet or sample test has been offered by the professor, make good use of it, above anything else, for the preparation for the test. Another great resource for getting to know the examination is reviewing tests from previous semesters. Use these tests to review, and aim to achieve a 100% score on each of the possible topics. With a few exceptions, the goal that you set for yourself is the highest one that you will reach.

Take all of the questions that were assigned as homework, and rework them to any other possible course material. The more problems reworked, the more skill and confidence will form as a result. When forming the solution to a problem, write out each of the steps. Don't simply do head work. By doing as many steps on paper as possible, much clarification and therefore confidence will be formed. Do this with as many homework problems as possible, before checking the answers. By checking the answer after each problem, a reinforcement will exist, that will not be on the exam. Study situations should be as exam-like as possible, to prime the test-taker's system for the experience. By waiting to check the answers at the end, a psychological advantage will be formed, to decrease the stress factor.

Another fantastic reason for not cramming is the avoidance of confusion in concepts, especially when it comes to mathematics. 8-10 hours of study will become one hundred percent more effective if it is spread out over a week or at least several days, instead of doing it all in one sitting. Recognize that the human brain requires time in order to assimilate new material, so frequent breaks and a span of study time over several days will be much more beneficial.

Additionally, don't study right up until the point of the exam. Studying should stop a minimum of one hour before the exam begins. This allows the brain to rest and put things in their proper order.  This will also provide the time to become as relaxed as possible when going into the examination room.  The test-taker will also have time to eat well and eat sensibly.  Know that the brain needs food as much as the rest of the body.  With enough food and enough sleep, as well as a relaxed attitude, the body and the mind are primed for success.

Avoid any anxious classmates who are talking about the exam.  These students only spread anxiety, and are not worth sharing the anxious sentimentalities.

Before the test also involves creating a positive attitude, so mental preparation should also be a point of concentration.  There are many keys to creating a positive attitude.  Should fears become rushing in, make a visualization of taking the exam, doing well, and seeing an A written on the paper.  Write out a list of affirmations that will bring a feeling of confidence, such as "I am doing well in my English class," "I studied well and know my material," "I enjoy this class."  Even if the affirmations aren't believed at first, it sends a positive message to the subconscious which will result in an alteration of the overall belief system, which is the system that creates reality.

If a sensation of panic begins, work with the fear and imagine the very worst!  Work through the entire scenario of not passing the test, failing the entire course, and dropping out of school, followed by not getting a job, and pushing a shopping cart through the dark alley where you'll live.  This will place things into perspective!  Then, practice deep breathing and create a visualization of the opposite situation - achieving an "A" on the exam, passing the entire course, receiving the degree at a graduation ceremony.

On the day of the test, there are many things to be done to ensure the best results, as well as the most calm outlook.  The following stages are suggested in order to maximize test-taking potential:

- Begin the examination day with a moderate breakfast, and avoid any coffee or beverages with caffeine if the test taker is prone to jitters.  Even people who are used to managing caffeine can feel jittery or light-headed when it is taken on a test day.
- Attempt to do something that is relaxing before the examination begins.  As last minute cramming clouds the mastering of overall concepts, it is better to use this time to create a calming outlook.
- Be certain to arrive at the test location well in advance, in order to provide time to select a location that is away from doors, windows and other distractions, as well as giving enough time to relax before the test begins.
- Keep away from anxiety generating classmates who will upset the sensation of stability and relaxation that is being attempted before the exam.
- Should the waiting period before the exam begins cause anxiety, create a self-distraction by reading a light magazine or something else that is relaxing and simple.

During the exam itself, read the entire exam from beginning to end, and find out how much time should be allotted to each individual problem.  Once writing the exam, should more time be taken for a problem, it should be abandoned, in order to begin another problem.  If there is time at the end, the unfinished problem can always be returned to and completed.

Read the instructions very carefully - twice - so that unpleasant surprises won't follow during or after the exam has ended.

When writing the exam, pretend that the situation is actually simply the completion of homework within a library, or at home. This will assist in forming a relaxed atmosphere, and will allow the brain extra focus for the complex thinking function.

Begin the exam with all of the questions with which the most confidence is felt. This will build the confidence level regarding the entire exam and will begin a quality momentum. This will also create encouragement for trying the problems where uncertainty resides.

Going with the "gut instinct" is always the way to go when solving a problem. Second guessing should be avoided at all costs. Have confidence in the ability to do well.

For essay questions, create an outline in advance that will keep the mind organized and make certain that all of the points are remembered. For multiple choice, read every answer, even if the correct one has been spotted - a better one may exist.

Continue at a pace that is reasonable and not rushed, in order to be able to work carefully. Provide enough time to go over the answers at the end, to check for small errors that can be corrected.

Should a feeling of panic begin, breathe deeply, and think of the feeling of the body releasing sand through its pores. Visualize a calm, peaceful place, and include all of the sights, sounds and sensations of this image. Continue the deep breathing, and take a few minutes to continue this with closed eyes. When all is well again, return to the test.

If a "blanking" occurs for a certain question, skip it and move on to the next question. There will be time to return to the other question later. Get everything done that can be done, first, to guarantee all the grades that can be compiled, and to build all of the confidence possible. Then return to the weaker questions to build the marks from there.

Remember, one's own reality can be created, so as long as the belief is there, success will follow. And remember: anxiety can happen later, right now, there's an exam to be written!

After the examination is complete, whether there is a feeling for a good grade or a bad grade, don't dwell on the exam, and be certain to follow through on the reward that was promised...and enjoy it! Don't dwell on any mistakes that have been made, as there is nothing that can be done at this point anyway.

Additionally, don't begin to study for the next test right away. Do something relaxing for a while, and let the mind relax and prepare itself to begin absorbing information again.

From the results of the exam - both the grade and the entire experience, be certain to learn from what has gone on. Perfect studying habits and work some more on confidence in order to make the next examination experience even better than the last one.

Learn to avoid places where openings occurred for laziness, procrastination and day dreaming.

Use the time between this exam and the next one to better learn to relax, even learning to relax on cue, so that any anxiety can be controlled during the next exam. Learn how to relax the body. Slouch in your chair if that helps. Tighten and then relax all of the different muscle groups, one group at a time, beginning with the feet and then working all the way up to the neck and face.

This will ultimately relax the muscles more than they were to begin with. Learn how to breathe deeply and comfortably, and focus on this breathing going in and out as a relaxing thought. With every exhale, repeat the word "relax."

As common as test anxiety is, it is very possible to overcome it. Make yourself one of the test-takers who overcome this frustrating hindrance.

# Special Report: Retaking the Test: What Are Your Chances at Improving Your Score?

After going through the experience of taking a major test, many test takers feel that once is enough. The test usually comes during a period of transition in the test taker's life, and taking the test is only one of a series of important events. With so many distractions and conflicting recommendations, it may be difficult for a test taker to rationally determine whether or not he should retake the test after viewing his scores.

The importance of the test usually only adds to the burden of the retake decision. However, don't be swayed by emotion. There a few simple questions that you can ask yourself to guide you as you try to determine whether a retake would improve your score:

1. What went wrong? Why wasn't your score what you expected?

Can you point to a single factor or problem that you feel caused the low score? Were you sick on test day? Was there an emotional upheaval in your life that caused a distraction? Were you late for the test or not able to use the full time allotment? If you can point to any of these specific, individual problems, then a retake should definitely be considered.

2. Is there enough time to improve?

Many problems that may show up in your score report may take a lot of time for improvement. A deficiency in a particular math skill may require weeks or months of tutoring and studying to improve. If you have enough time to improve an identified weakness, then a retake should definitely be considered.

3. How will additional scores be used? Will a score average, highest score, or most recent score be used?

Different test scores may be handled completely differently. If you've taken the test multiple times, sometimes your highest score is used, sometimes your average score is computed and used, and sometimes your most recent score is used. Make sure you understand what method will be used to evaluate your scores, and use that to help you determine whether a retake should be considered.

4. Are my practice test scores significantly higher than my actual test score?

If you have taken a lot of practice tests and are consistently scoring at a much higher level than your actual test score, then you should consider a retake. However, if you've taken five practice tests and only one of your scores was higher than your actual test score, or if your practice test scores were only slightly higher than your actual test score, then it is unlikely that you will significantly increase your score.

5. Do I need perfect scores or will I be able to live with this score? Will this score still allow me to follow my dreams?

What kind of score is acceptable to you? Is your current score "good enough?" Do you have to have a certain score in order to pursue the future of your dreams? If you won't be happy with your current score, and there's no way that you could live with it, then you should consider a retake. However, don't get your hopes up. If you are looking for significant improvement, that may or may not be possible. But if you won't be happy otherwise, it is at least worth the effort.

Remember that there are other considerations. To achieve your dream, it is likely that your grades may also be taken into account. A great test score is usually not the only thing necessary to succeed. Make sure that you aren't overemphasizing the importance of a high test score.

Furthermore, a retake does not always result in a higher score. Some test takers will score lower on a retake, rather than higher. One study shows that one-fourth of test takers will achieve a significant improvement in test score, while one-sixth of test takers will actually show a decrease. While this shows that most test takers will improve, the majority will only improve their scores a little and a retake may not be worth the test taker's effort.

Finally, if a test is taken only once and is considered in the added context of good grades on the part of a test taker, the person reviewing the grades and scores may be tempted to assume that the test taker just had a bad day while taking the test, and may discount the low test score in favor of the high grades. But if the test is retaken and the scores are approximately the same, then the validity of the low scores are only confirmed. Therefore, a retake could actually hurt a test taker by definitely bracketing a test taker's score ability to a limited range.

# Additional Bonus Material

Due to our efforts to try to keep this book to a manageable length, we've created a link that will give you access to all of your additional bonus material.

Please visit http://www.mometrix.com/bonus948/ssatmiddle to access the information.